KT-512-647

WARWICK LIBRARY SCHOOL

THE ARAB–ISRAELI CONFLICT

The Library at Warwick School
Please return or renew on or before the last date below

3/13

Campus Library Services Limited
68243

WARWICK SCHOOL

The Arab–Israeli Conflict

KIRSTEN E. SCHULZE

LONGMAN
LONDON AND NEW YORK

Pearson Education Limited,
Edinburgh Gate,
Harlow,
Essex CM20 2JE,
United Kingdom
and Associated Companies throughout the world.

Visit us on the World Wide Web at:
www.pearsoned.co.uk

© Addison Wesley Longman Limited 1999

The right of Kirsten Schulze to be identified as the author
of this work has been asserted by her in accordance with
the Copyright, Designs and Patents Act 1988.

All rights reserved; no part of this publication may be
reproduced, stored in a retrieval system, or transmitted
in any form or by any means, electronic, mechanical,
photocopying, recording, or otherwise without either the
prior written permission of the Publishers or a licence
permitting restricted copying in the United Kingdom
issued by the Copyright Licensing Agency Ltd.,
90 Tottenham Court Road, London W1T 4LP

First published 1999

ISBN-10: 0-582-31646-4
ISBN-13: 978-0-582-31646-1

Visit Addison Wesley Longman on the world wide web at http://www.awl-he.com

British Library Cataloguing-in-Publication Data
A catalogue record for this book is available from the British Library

Library of Congress Cataloging-in-Publication Data
Schulze, Kirsten E.
    The Arab-Israeli conflict / Kirsten E. Schultze.
        p.   cm. – (Seminar studies in history)
    Includes bibliographical references and index.
    ISBN 0-582-31646-4
    1. Arab-Israeli conflict. 2. Arab-Israeli conflict – 1993 – Peace.
I. Title.   II. Series.
DS119.7.S37935   1999
956.05′3–dc21
                                                        98-46953
12 11 10   CIP
08 07 06 05

Set by 7 in 10/12 Sabon
Printed in Malaysia, PP

CONTENTS

AN INTRODUCTION TO THE SERIES

Such is the pace of historical enquiry in the modern world that there is an ever-widening gap between the specialist article or monograph, incorporating the results of current research, and general surveys, which inevitably become out of date. *Seminar Studies in History* are designed to bridge this gap. The series was founded by Patrick Richardson in 1966 and his aim was to cover major themes in British, European and World history. Between 1980 and 1996 Roger Lockyer continued his work, before handing the editorship over to Clive Emsley and Gordon Martel. Clive Emsley is Professor of History at the Open University, while Gordon Martel is Professor of International History at the University of Northern British Columbia, Canada and Senior Research Fellow at De Montfort University.

All the books are written by experts in their field who are not only familiar with the latest research but have often contributed to it. They are frequently revised, in order to take account of new information and interpretations. They provide a selection of documents to illustrate major themes and provoke discussion, and also a guide to further reading. The aim of *Seminar Studies* is to clarify complex issues without over-simplifying them, and to stimulate readers into deepening their knowledge and understanding of major themes and topics.

NOTE ON REFERENCING SYSTEM

Readers should note that numbers in square brackets [5] refer them to the corresponding entry in the Bibliography at the end of the book (specific page numbers are given in italics). A number in square brackets preceded by *Doc.* [*Doc. 5*] refers readers to the corresponding item in the Documents section which follows the main text. Words and abbreviations asterisked at first occurrence are defined in the Glossary.

LIST OF MAPS

ACKNOWLEDGEMENTS

No book is ever the product of one person alone. So I would like to thank the following friends and colleagues for their comments, suggestions and support: Fred Halliday, Avraham Sela, Abigail, Rona, Catherine, Melissa, Elizabeth, Kate, Gary, Yussi and Tim. Moreover, I am grateful to my students for making the Arab–Israeli conflict a subject worth teaching and writing about.

The publishers would like to thank the following for permission to reproduce copyright material:

Indiana University Press for extracts from *The Evolution of the Army's Role in Strategic Planning* by Amir Bar-Or, published in *Israel Studies* vol. 1 no. 2 1996; extracts from *Arab–Israeli Conflict and Conciliation: a Documentary Record* edited by B. Reich, 1995, published by Preager, an imprint of Greenwood Publishing Group, Inc., Westport, CT, USA; and Routledge Publishers for two revised maps from *Atlas of the Arab–Israeli Conflict* by M Gilbert, 1993.

Whilst every effort has been made to trace the owners of copyright material, in a few cases this has proved to be problematic and so we take this opportunity to offer our apologies to any copyright holders whose rights we may have unwittingly infringed.

This book is dedicated to the memory of my grandparents
Gladys Witter Lovell
and
John Wallace Lovell

PART ONE: BACKGROUND

1 THE ORIGINS OF THE ARAB–ISRAELI CONFLICT

The origins of the Arab–Israeli conflict have been the subject of numerous debates. Biblical enmity between Abraham's two sons Isaac and Ishmael, the advent of Islam, the prophet Mohammed's quarrel with the Jews of Medina, the emergence of Zionism in the nineteenth century, and British colonial policy in the early twentieth century have all been considered appropriate starting points. While a case for these points of departure can be made, it will be argued here that the Arab–Israeli conflict emerged with the advent of nationalism in the Middle East and that the conflict, in simplistic terms, is one of competing nationalisms.

ZIONISM AND ARAB NATIONALISM

Zionism and Arab nationalism embarked upon a course of parallel development in the nineteenth century as predominantly secular political ideologies based on emancipation and self-determination. Both started in intellectual circles as a response to challenges from Europe during that period [136], and both evolved around the concepts of identity, nationhood, history, religion and culture.

Classical Zionism was rooted in the traditional ties Jews in the Diaspora* proclaimed to the Land of Israel, and the belief that Jewish independence would be restored with the coming of the Messiah. Within the framework of the European enlightenment, the French Revolution, and new concepts of citizenship and political life, and against the backdrop of centuries of inequality and persecution, classical Zionism started to be transformed into modern political Zionism [78]. The ideological foundation for modern political Zionism was as follows: the Jewish people constituted a nation and this nationhood needed to be reaffirmed; assimilation was rejected as it was neither desirable nor was it deemed to be possible; anti-Semitism could only be overcome by physical separation from Europe and by self-determination;

and religious and cultural ties to the Land of Israel made Palestine the logical territorial claim.

One of the key Zionist thinkers was Theodor Herzl, a journalist and playwright from Vienna, Austria. His main contribution to Zionism was his book *Der Judenstaat* (*The Jewish State*), published in 1896, which, as its name implies, advocated independent statehood. The creation of a Jewish state in Palestine was the only viable and permanent solution to the problem of the Jews. Through a state of their own, the Jewish people could finally occupy an equal place among nations. Herzl's activism and his ideas resulted in the establishment of the Zionist Organisation and the convening of the First Zionist Congress in 1897 in Basle, Switzerland. Through this institutional basis modern Zionism evolved from a small intellectual movement into an international movement. The promotion of Jewish immigration to Palestine and the acquisition of land were its two most important objectives.

Immigration to Palestine up to this point had been sporadic, and with the exception of the Bilu group in 1882 who are considered to be the first *Aliyah* (immigration wave), was an expression of individual commitment. The Zionist institutional framework was now able to organise immigration as well as to lay the foundations for the *Yishuv** (Jewish settlement) in Palestine. The second *Aliyah** started in 1904 and lasted until 1913. Most of the new immigrants were of Russian and East European origin, having fled persecution following the 1905 aborted Russian revolution. An estimated 2.5 million Jews left Russia at that time, of which 60,000 settled in Palestine [136]. This second wave of immigrants is generally credited with creating the first institutions in Palestine and thus the beginning of proto-state formation. Their most famous achievement was the agricultural co-operative or *kibbutz**.

Zionism as a modern nationalist movement came into direct competition with Arab nationalism and later with Palestinian nationalism, as both Jews and Arabs laid claim to the same territory. Arab nationalism is the belief that the Arab people constitute a single political community or nation, which should be either independent and united under a common government [54] or a set of independent allied Arab states. Modern Arab nationalism emerged within the context of the Arab renaissance or awakening which began at the end of the eighteenth century. This renaissance was in part a response to the challenge of modernisation but also an engagement with European nationalist ideas of freedom, independence, equality and progress. Arab nationalism embodied both elements, embracing modernisation but at the same time stressing that European colonialism was super-fluous in its attainment [136].

Like Zionism, Arab nationalism started to develop in intellectual circles. The first Arab nationalist party, in fact, was a small secret society founded around 1875 by graduates of the American University of Beirut. Other societies and literary clubs soon followed and disseminated Arab national ideas of unity, language and culture.

At the core of Arab nationalism, like any other nationalism, was the concept of self-determination. This quest for independence emphasised three elements in Arab nationalism. First, there was a strong anti-Turkish sentiment as a reaction to centuries of Ottoman control but also to the 1908 Young Turks revolution. Secondly, the entrance of European colonial powers and foreign control of Arab land led to an anti-colonial and anti-imperial element. Thirdly, the interaction and competition with Zionism also provided it with an anti-Zionist ideology.

Despite these common aims the Arab nationalist movement was by no means unified. Not only did it have to contend with differing views on the degree of autonomy and the type of political system the Arab people should aim for, but it also had to deal with leadership contests and the emergence of separate localised nationalisms. A distinct Palestinian nationalism was one such split. However, that did not start to develop until Palestine came under British mandate, and Jewish immigration and institution-building became perceived as a threat to the local Arab population.

Arab nationalism was as much shaped by its environment, and particularly Western political events, as Zionism was. For instance, the first Arab Congress was organised in 1913 in Paris – not in the Middle East. The aims of the congress at that time were the establishment of administrative autonomy, Arab participation in the Ottoman central government, making Arabic an official language, and generally striving towards unity – but all still within the framework of the already disintegrating Ottoman Empire. Other Arab nationalists, however, demanded full independence, a demand for which the outbreak of the First World War and the defeat of the Ottoman Empire would provide the perfect opportunity.

THE IMPACT OF THE FIRST WORLD WAR

The outbreak of the First World War in 1914 ushered in important changes for the achievement of both Arab nationalist and Zionist aspirations, mainly as a result of Britain's policy of alliances. The

Ottoman Empire had entered the war on the side of Germany. This meant that in the Middle East Britain was effectively fighting the Ottoman. In order to prevent the latter from taking the Suez Canal, Britain started to cultivate local Arab allies who would aid its war effort [54]. In 1915 the British High Commissioner in Cairo, Sir Henry McMahon, negotiated the support of the Hashemite* leader and the Amir of Mecca, Sharif Hussein, in return for the promise of future Arab independence. Embodied in a set of letters known as the Hussein–McMahon Correspondence [*Doc. 1*] is the promise that the Arab territory of the Ottoman Empire be returned to Arab sovereignty, with the exception of the districts of Mersina and Alexandretta as well as the districts west of Damascus, Homs, Hama and Aleppo, which were not purely Arab. The excluded territory, according to Arab interpretation, referred to present-day Lebanon and parts of Syria only. It did not include Palestine, despite Britain's later claim that it did.

The promise of Arab independence and statehood was not the only British pledge made in the context of First World War alliance policy. By the summer of 1917 the British government had also started to consider the Zionist movement as a potential ally [47]. The key player on the Zionist side was the Russian-born chemist Chaim Weizmann who was teaching at Manchester University. Before the war he had already had contact with a number of liberal and conservative politicians, including former Prime Minister Arthur Balfour. Weizmann furthered Zionist aspirations in two important ways: first, he was an excellent diplomat and eloquent spokesperson for the movement; secondly, he was involved in the synthesising of acetone, hitherto imported from Germany, and essential for making explosives and consequently for Britain's war effort. Both enabled him to convince British decision-makers that the Zionists were important for Britain's war effort. The Zionists could help sustain the Russian front which was collapsing from internal Russian revolutionary turmoil, and they could help galvanise the desperately needed American war effort. The result of Weizmann's diplomacy and powers of persuasion was a declaration issued by Foreign Secretary Balfour on 2 November 1917, stating that 'His Majesty's Government viewed with favour the establishment in Palestine of a national home for the Jewish people.' [*Doc. 2*]

Some observations should be made at this point. The Balfour Declaration did not state that Palestine should be turned into a Jewish state. In fact, the word 'state' had initially appeared in the earlier drafts of the statement but was changed due to pressure from British Jews who feared that this would prejudice their rights and citizenship within the United Kingdom. Further, neither the Balfour Declaration nor the Hussein–McMahon Correspondence were specific about the actual borders of the territory promised to both Jews and Arabs. The result was that both Zionists and Arab nationalists believed Palestine had been promised to them; the seeds for conflict had been sown.

BRITISH POLICY AND THE PALESTINE MANDATE

British troops entered Palestine in 1918 and set up a provisional military government in Jerusalem. Britain had thus physically laid claim to a territory not only promised to the Arabs and Zionists, but also to one designated as an international zone in the secret 1916 British–French Sykes–Picot Agreement [*Doc. 3*]. Anticipating the future dismemberment of the Ottoman Empire, Britain and France had carved the Middle East into spheres of influence to prevent a power vacuum and Russian entry into the region. British military presence from 1918 onwards assured Britain that it was granted the mandate over Palestine by the League of Nations in 1922, fulfilling its strategic aims of 'assuring access to the Suez Canal and the East, preventing French ambitions in Lebanon and Syria from drifting South, and creating a land bridge from the Mediterranean Sea to the oil fields of Iraq' [134 *p. 7*]. The mandate provided Britain with the responsibility for placing the country under 'such political, administrative, and economic conditions as will secure the establishment of the Jewish national home ... and the development of self-governing institutions, and also for safeguarding the civil and religious rights of all the inhabitants of Palestine, irrespective of race and religion.'

British policy was caught between conflicting promises and different views within its own establishment right from the beginning. Popular perception of this period is that Britain was a more than inadequate mandate power which managed to stir up Arab resentment and at the same time was hostile to the Zionist state-building project. A policy acceptable to both Arabs and Zionists was never achieved and British policy on the ground was further complicated by often contradictory positions in world politics. For instance, in the international arena Britain tended to support Zionism, while in Palestine, British officials favoured the Arabs, often influenced by concern for Muslim opinion in neighbouring countries and India [54]. Arab and Jewish suspicions of each other and of British intentions flourished in such an environment. Many Arabs believed that Britain was planning to hold on to Palestine until a Jewish majority had been achieved. Many Jews believed that Britain was secretly aiding and arming the Arabs as well restricting Jewish immigration and land purchases in order to prevent the creation of a Jewish state. While British Palestine policy stumbled from one crisis to another, inter-communal violence rose, starting with the first Arab disturbances in 1920 and 1921.

THE INTER-WAR PERIOD

The period between the two World Wars was characterised by institution-building in Palestine. Britain's first civilian governor, Sir Herbert Samuel, encouraged both Jews and Arabs to form their own institutions. The Zionist Commission which had been established after the Balfour Declaration evolved into the Palestine Zionist Executive in 1920 and became the Jewish Agency* in 1928–29. Foundations laid earlier by the Zionist Organisation were expanded and built upon. The majority of institutions which later served as the framework for the new Israeli state, were established during this time, including political parties, the general labour federation or *Histadrut**, the underground defence organisation or *Haganah**, and the Hebrew University of Jerusalem. These institutions constituted a proto-state which made the transition to full statehood in 1948 easier.

Arab or indeed Palestinian institution-building did not take place at the same rate. Despite the fact that the British military and civil administration encouraged Palestinian Arabs to mobilise, resulting in the formation of the Arab Executive in 1920, the Arabs remained divided by religious, family and regional loyalties. Consequently the local Arab Executive was a feeble vehicle for their aspirations, beset by feuds between followers of the two leading notable Jerusalem families, the Husseinis and Nashashibis, who, amongst other issues, were split over the degree of Arab co-operation with the British authorities. In the 1930s the feud was clearly won by the Mufti of Jerusalem, Hajj Amin al-Husseini, who emerged as the unrivalled leader of the Palestinian cause. In addition to local rivalry, the emergence of Palestinian nationalism which needed to counter the advances of the Zionist project on the ground, competed directly with the Arab nationalist agenda promoted by the Hashemites.

In the early days under Samuel it looked as if Jewish–Arab differences would be resolved in the near future. The number of Jewish immigrants had started to decrease, and some immigrants decided to leave Palestine for the greener shores of the United States [54 *p. 248*]. A limited amount of Arab–Jewish co-operation and the absence of widespread violence supported this perception. In 1929, however, the situation changed drastically with the Wailing Wall* incident. The disturbances which erupted in response to benches being set up in front of the Wailing Wall resulted in 133 Jewish deaths and 116 Arab deaths [47 *p. 11*]. It was followed by the massacre of most of the Jewish residents of Hebron. The British attempt to calm the situation further exacerbated inter-communal tension. Colonial Secretary Lord Passfield issued a White Paper blaming the Jewish Agency land purchases for the disturbances. Restrictions on Jewish immigrants were consequently tightened. The Jewish reaction was outrage. In an attempt to assuage the Jews, the British Prime Minister Ramsay Mac-Donald then issued a letter explaining away the White Paper, which, in turn, angered the Arabs.

During the 1930s British policy started to shift from the 'status of umpire to that of advocate and finally paternal defender of Arab rights' [134 *p. 81*]. At the same time the rise to power of Adolf Hitler in Germany and his anti-Semitic ideology made the Zionist need for a Jewish state more pressing. Restrictions on immigration into the United States left Palestine as the only alternative. The number of Jewish immigrants started to increase again. Between 1930 and 1936 alone the Jewish population rose from 164,000 to 370,000. Thus it is no surprise that the local Arab population became more and more convinced that their aspirations would ultimately be sacrificed for German ambitions. This feeling of anger and impotence among the Arabs led to a new phase in Arab nationalism, which can be seen as the first popular expression of a distinctly Palestinian nationalism.

Arab opposition to this increased immigration found expression in the Arab Revolt, which began on 15 April 1936 with the murder of a Jew near the town of Nablus. The Arab Higher Committee was formed under the leadership of Hajj Amin al-Husseini and found support in the wider Arab nationalist community. The initial strike turned into a large-scale rebellion, paralysing Palestine for months. The revolt tied up British military resources at a time when belligerence was increasing in Europe. An end to the Arab Revolt had to be achieved in order to avoid being caught in a two-front war. The Palestine Royal Commission was set up under Lord Peel in order to determine the causes of the conflict and find a way of dealing with the grievances of both Arabs and Jews. The Arabs, however, boycotted the Commission until just before its departure, effectively leaving the floor to the Zionists. In 1937 the Commission published its recommendations [*Doc. 4*], stating that co-existence was impossible and that partition was the only solution. Arab opposition to partition was inevitable, and as war in Europe was only a matter of time, the good-will of the Arabs needed to be re-established quickly. Colonial Secretary

Malcolm MacDonald thus issued a White Paper in 1939 [*Doc. 5*], which not only limited Jewish immigration to 15,000 per year until 1944 but also made it contingent upon Arab consent thereafter. For the Jews the 1939 White Paper represented the deepest act of betrayal at the time of their greatest peril [*47 p. 14*]. It ensured that the limited of number of Jews who were able to escape the death camps of the Holocaust had nowhere to go.

THE IMPACT OF THE SECOND WORLD WAR

The Second World War broke out when the German army invaded Poland on 1 September 1939. As most Arab countries were still under some form of mandate control at that time, the official Arab position was one of neutrality. Arab sentiments in Palestine, however, were more ambiguous. Hajj Amin al-Husseini had made contacts with Germany, seeing the Nazis as a tool to free Palestine from both the British and the Zionists. The Germans, conversely, saw Husseini as a vehicle for recruiting Bosnian Muslims into the SS. While Husseini's decision not to remain neutral was by choice, neutrality for the Jews was an option not afforded them. The unravelling events in Germany and Eastern Europe made it imperative for the Jews to join the Allied war effort. Palestinian Jews enlisted in the British Army in large numbers despite their resentment against British policy in Palestine. Zionist leader and future prime minister of Israel, David Ben Gurion, summed up the Jewish attitude in Palestine quite aptly when he said: 'We must assist the British in the war as if there were no White Paper and we must resist the White Paper as if there were no war' [*54 p. 251*].

Assistance in the war came through the contribution of a Jewish legion, which fought alongside the British Army in the Middle East and Europe [50]. Resisting the White Paper came in the form of illegal immigration. In 1940 alone an estimated 40,000 Jews entered Palestine illegally [*147 p. 47*]. British reaction was to suspend the quota allowed under the White Paper in October 1940, and to intercept ships and deport refugees. The stream of immigrants declined sharply in 1941 when Germany gained control of the Balkans, but increased again with the end of the war and the liberation of the concentration camps. Britain's attempts to stifle immigration resulted in the confiscation of ships, preventing ships from sailing by diplomatic means, intercepting ships and diverting them to Cyprus [57] – a policy pursued until the expiry of the mandate.

The Second World War had a number of dramatic effects upon the conflict in Palestine. First, Britain's empire was clearly in decline.

Maintaining colonies, protectorates and mandates was becoming increasingly in the face of the worsening economic situation in the United Kingdom. Maintaining the Palestine mandate and containing the increasing conflict were becoming too costly, politically, economically and financially, at a time when the British government's priority was post-war reconstruction. Thus, from 1945 onwards, Britain started to look for an honourable way out.

Secondly, concomitant with the decline of British influence was the rise of US influence in the region. Lobbying by Jewish Americans and a broad American-Zionist network resulted in the Biltmore Program at a conference in May 1942 which called for a Jewish state in Palestine. This programme did not find immediate support within the US administration, as President Roosevelt was worried about Arab oil supplies during the war. Yet, in the 1944 presidential elections, keeping the ethnic vote in mind, both Democratic and Republican election platforms endorsed the Biltmore Program. The stage for post-war US policy had been set.

Thirdly, the Holocaust and the mass murder of 5,600,000–6,900,000 Jews led the survivors of the camps and the Zionist Movement to push even harder for a state. It had become clear that only a state of their own could provide the Jews with security. The Holocaust also engendered international sympathy, which the Zionist cause needed for the final stage in its struggle for statehood.

Fourthly, as a result of the war Europe was faced with a refugee problem of enormous proportions. This created pressure for increasing the number of Jewish immigrants to Palestine and for ending the restrictions on land purchases. These two issues were the key recommendations of the 1946 Anglo-American Committee of Inquiry.

And fifthly, the situation in Palestine had deteriorated rapidly towards the end of the war and had developed into an almost full-scale Jewish uprising against the British, as well as inter-communal Arab–Jewish tensions bordering on civil war. By October 1947, Jewish attacks had killed 127 British soldiers and wounded 133 others [50 *p. 52*]. British policy had become untenable.

These five key factors created the environment which made British withdrawal almost inevitable and the establishment of a Jewish state in Palestine possible. It also convinced both Jews and Arabs that ultimately there would be war.

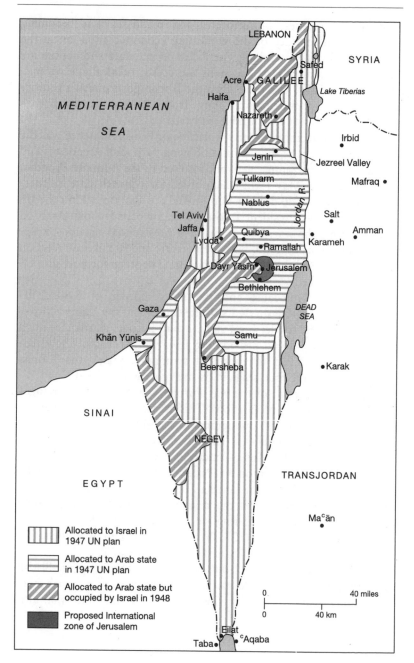

Map 1   Palestine and Transjordan, 1947–48

THE BRITISH WITHDRAWAL FROM PALESTINE

The British withdrawal from Palestine and the decision to hand Palestine over to the newly established United Nations was the result of Britain's inability to settle the conflict between Zionists and Arabs as well as Britain's need to address more pressing matters at home. The United Nations set up a Special Committee for Palestine (UNSCOP)* and sent it on a mission of inquiry during the summer of 1947. Like the 1937 Peel Commission and the 1946 Anglo-American Commission, UNSCOP set out to listen to both Arabs and Jews in Palestine as well as to consider the submissions of other Arab leaders of the region. But believing that the Commission was already biased towards the Zionists, the Arab Higher Committee boycotted it. This Arab perception was to some extent correct, as the visible horrors of the Holocaust and the alliance of Haj Amin al-Husseini with Adolf Hitler had already reduced UNSCOP's choice [100]. These perceptions, however, were only reinforced by the Arab boycott.

Like the previous commissions, UNSCOP too came to the conclusion that both Jewish and Arab claims were of equal validity, that their aspirations were irreconcilable, and that the only viable solution to the conflict was the separation of the two communities by partitioning the territory and creating both an Arab and a Jewish state.

The Partition Plan drawn up by UNSCOP divided Palestine in accordance with the existing settlement pattern and population centres. The proposed Arab state was to consist of the coastal strip of Gaza, the Galilee in the north, and the area around Nablus, Hebron and Beersheba. The proposed Jewish state was to consist of the coastal area around Tel Aviv and Haifa, the Negev in the south, and the Jezreel and Hule valleys. The city of Jerusalem, according to the UN partition plan, was to come under international control [*Map 1*]. One problem with the plan was the territorial fragmentation of both proposed states, as well as the notion that while partition was necessary, economic unity should be retained. Another problem was the Arab population 'trapped' in the proposed Jewish state.

While Zionist politicians did not like the status of Jerusalem or the lack of territorial contiguity, they accepted the plan as a first step to statehood. The Arab leadership, on the other hand, could not find any redeeming aspects in a plan that allotted part of their territory to the Zionists. Arab League* members met to adopt a common strategy and decided to go to war to prevent the creation of a Jewish state. Beyond the public facade of unity, however, Arab leaders were as divided as ever. King Abdallah of Transjordan concluded a secret deal with the Zionists to partition the Arab sections of Palestine [128].

Egypt and Syria also had territorial as well as leadership ambitions. When the Partition Plan was passed in the General Assembly on 25 November 1947 by a vote of 33 in favour, 13 against (including the United Kingdom) and 10 abstentions, it was not surprising that the five Arab member states opposed it.

Immediately following the General Assembly vote, both Jews and Arabs started to arm themselves. The Arab Higher Committee called a strike for 2–4 December which sparked off the first inter-communal clashes. The British mandate authorities in the meantime were biding their time until complete withdrawal, unable and unwilling to either curb the ensuing civil war or implement partition. The months before the end of the mandate were characterised by bitter fighting – including the massacre at the Arab village of Deir Yassin by the Irgun* and Lehi which killed 250, the Arab ambush on a Jewish medical convoy killing 75, and the Arab siege of Jerusalem – ultimately resulting in a mass exodus of Palestine's Arabs [92].

On 14 May 1948 the Jewish Agency declared the territory allotted to the Jews as the new state of Israel. The next day Egyptian, Lebanese, Jordanian, Syrian and Iraqi troops attacked the fledgling Jewish state to 'liberate Palestine'. The contest for Palestine and conflicting communal aspirations had turned into what is known as the Arab–Israeli Conflict.

PART TWO: WARS AND PEACE

2   THE 1948 WAR

The debate surrounding the events of 1948, the creation of the state of Israel, the Arab defeat and the Palestinian refugee problem, becomes apparent with the way the war is referred to in Israeli and Arab historiography. For Israelis it was the War of Independence, for the Arab states it was the Palestine War, and for the Palestinians it became known as 'the disaster' – an-Nakba*. Attempts to apportion responsibility for the refugee situation, the conduct of forces during the war, and the inability to reach a peaceful settlement in its aftermath, have resulted in controversy between traditionalist and revisionist historians in Israel, as well as disputes between Arab, Israeli and Palestinian scholars and politicians.

THE FIRST ARAB–ISRAELI WAR

Israel's declaration of independence [Doc. 7] on 14 May 1948 was immediately followed by the declaration of war by five Arab states, turning the on-going Zionist–Palestinian civil war into an Arab–Israeli inter-state conflict. An estimated 6,000–7,000 Arab volunteers constituting the Arab Liberation Army* [136 p. 263] achieved a number of early successes. From the outbreak of the war on 30 November 1947 until June 1948, Israel was fighting for survival. Problems of arms procurement, difficulties of co-ordinating an army consisting of European refugees and local Jews, and numeric inferiority were making themselves felt. The Arab campaign along major roads was threatening the existence of outlying Jewish settlements as well as the supply line to the larger Jewish towns. The situation for the new state of Israel was particularly critical in the Galilee where Jewish settlements were surrounded by Arab villages, as well as in Jerusalem where the Jewish population was almost completely under siege and running out of food, water and ammunition. It was with this situation in mind that the controversial Plan D or Dalet* [Doc. 6] was drafted to secure the fledgling state and defend outlying settlements. 'The battle against the local and foreign irregulars had to be won first if there was to be a chance of defeating the invading regular Arab armies. To win the battle of the roads, the *Haganah* had to pacify the Arab villages and towns that dominated them: pacification perforce meant either the surrender of the villages or their depopulation and destruction' [92 *p. 62*]. The main question Plan *Dalet* raises is to what extent the plan constituted a blueprint for the expulsion of the Palestinian Arabs and can be seen as the cause of the Palestinian refugee problem.

The aim of the intervention of the Arab states in the Palestinian–Israeli conflict was officially the liberation of Palestine. A closer look at Arab war aims, however, reveals that they were not united and that each state was pursuing its own political and territorial aims. One motive for Arab intervention, for instance, was to pre-empt Transjordan's King Abdallah from laying claim to the Arab parts of Palestine. Egypt and Syria, too, had their eyes on expansion rather than establishing a Palestinian state. The result of these separate aims was lack of unity, failure to co-ordinate battle plans, and lack of integration of the respective armies. In addition, except for Transjordan's Arab Legion*, the Arab armies were generally poorly trained and badly equipped [104]. In fact, morale was so low that only a month later, in June, the Arab campaign to liberate Palestine had lost its momentum.

The turning point in the war came on 11 June 1948 with the first truce ordered by the UN Security Council* and supervised by UN mediator Count Folke Bernadotte. Bernadotte proposed a new political compromise, calling for a Palestine Union to consist of separate Jewish, Palestinian and Transjordanian* units. This proposal, however, was not acceptable to any party to the conflict. By that time, Israel had attained numerical superiority. In mid-May Arab troops were estimated at 20,000–25,000 while the Israel Defence Force (IDF)* had mobilised 65,000. By September that number had risen to 90,000, and by December it peaked at 96,441 [130 *p. 294*]. Moreover, during this truce Israel was able to import a significant amount of rifles, machine guns, armoured cars, field guns, tanks and ammunition, despite the UN embargo. The combination of increased manpower and firepower tipped the balance decidedly in Israel's favour. Between the resumption of fighting on 8 July and the second truce on 19 July, Israeli forces seized Nazareth. Both sides, as before, violated the terms of this truce. By December 1948 Israel was able to break the Egyptian blockade in the Negev, to seize most of the Galilee, and cross the border into southern Lebanon while Bernadotte continued to promote compromise. In light of Israeli territorial gains, his efforts were perceived as pro-Arab, and he was consequently shot by members of the Jewish underground organisation *Lehi* on 17 September 1948 [104].

Armistice negotiations began in January 1949, when it became clear that the Arab states could not win the war. Israel's victory and the defeat of the Arab armies were the result of a number of factors: Israeli troops were highly motivated. They were also better trained, as many officers and enlisted personnel had gained combat experience in the British army during the Second World War. The Arab armies, in comparison, were ill-equipped, had logistical problems, lacked morale, and their leadership was divided.

The post-1948 war changes to the region were quite dramatic. Not only was Israel there to stay, but during the course of the war it had increased its territory to such an extent that a contiguous and therefore defensible border had been created [see *Map 1*]. Israel had increased its territory by 21 per cent compared with the partition resolution boundaries. Its demographic make-up comprised 716,700 Jews, of which 591,400 were of European (Ashkenazi*) origin and 105,000 were of Oriental (Sephardi*) origin, as well as 165,000 Arabs, of which 19 per cent were Christian and 10 per cent Druze* and Circassian* [50 p. 74]. The Arab states, too, had increased their territory, revealing that the Arab states had not been motivated by solidarity with the Palestinians but were competing with each other for power and territory. Transjordan gained the West Bank and Egypt the Gaza Strip. The Palestinians in contrast had lost any possibility of a state of their own. The defeat of the Arab states had important domestic repercussions as well. It de-legitimised the existing leadership, leading to revolutions, military coups and instability. Last but not least, the Palestinian Arab population had been divided: 150,000 came under Israeli rule and were granted Israeli citizenship, 450,000 came under Transjordanian control becoming Jordanian citizens, and 200,000 came under Egyptian control. The total number of Palestinian refugees at the end of 1948 was somewhere between 550,000 and 800,000.

THE PALESTINIAN REFUGEE PROBLEM

When fighting broke out following the UN partition resolution, Palestinians started to leave their homes in areas directly affected by the inter-communal violence. Middle- and upper-class families were the first to leave for neighbouring countries. Their departure was considered temporary, as they hoped to return to their homes after the fighting had died down. The Palestinian exodus was accelerated after the

Deir Yassin massacre and the Palestinian broadcast which followed it. The Palestine National Committee under the leadership of Dr Hussein Fakhri El Khalidi attempted to make Arab governments send troops by exaggerating the Deir Yassin atrocities in a subsequent radio broadcast. 'We want you to say that the Jews slaughtered people, committed atrocities, raped, and stole gold' [23, *p. 33*]. The broadcast had a devastating impact on everyone in Palestine, and the exodus began. It was retrospectively described as the biggest blunder that could have happened. When the Arab states finally invaded Israel, 200,000 [104 *p. 44*] Palestinians had already left. After the war, the UN estimated the total refugee population at 750,000 by the beginning of 1949, and 940,000 by June of that year, coming from 369 Palestinian towns and villages.

There are three main points of contention with regard to the refugee issue. The first is a dispute over how many Palestinians left. Estimates vary greatly from one source to another, whereby Israeli sources have tended to underestimate and Arab sources have tended to overestimate the numbers. Both sides, however, concur that only about 150,000 Palestinians remained inside Israel [136]. The second point of contention concerns the circumstances surrounding the Palestinian exodus. Israel has blamed the Arab states for the departure of the Palestinians, maintaining that the invading Arab armies had urged the Palestinians to temporarily vacate their villages in order to smooth the path for the advancing troops. The Arabs, in turn, charged Israel with expulsion of the Palestinians as part of a systematic campaign of ethnic cleansing. Both accounts are true to some degree. While there may not have been a Zionist plan for systematic expulsion, there were cases such as the Lydda and Ramle expulsion campaigns. On the other hand there were also examples such as Haifa where the Jews pleaded with Arab residents not to flee, or where Arab residents after surrender were permitted to stay, such as in Nazareth. Similarly, on the Arab side, there is evidence of local Arab leaders encouraging flight, but no official call upon the Palestinians to evacuate the area for the advancing Arab armies. Indeed, the Palestinian exodus developed a momentum of its own driven by war, fear, massacres, Arab encouragement and Zionist intimidation.

This leads directly to the third issue of solutions to the refugee problem. Attributing responsibility for the refugee problem was crucial as it ultimately determined whether these refugees would be permitted to return to their homes or had to resettle in the neighbouring Arab states. The Arabs demanded that the Palestinian refugees should return to their homes – after all, Israel had illegally expelled them.

Israel, conversely, maintained that the Palestinians should be integrated into the Arab states – after all, they had left voluntarily. Moreover, Jews living in Arab countries had migrated to Israel after 1948, so there had been a population exchange [136]. Ultimately, because Israel felt it could not realistically re-admit hundreds of thousands of Palestinians without placing at risk political and economic stability as well as the Jewish character of the state, Israel did not permit the refugees to return. As a result, the refugee problem became one of the most important issues for future attempts at negotiating Arab–Israeli peace.

Palestinian refugees emigrated to the Persian Gulf, Europe and North America. Some were integrated into the business communities of neighbouring Arab capitals such as Beirut, Amman, Damascus and Cairo. However, most of them settled in camps close to the Israeli border or on the outskirts of major Arab cities. The inability and to some extent unwillingness of the Arab states to absorb these refugees, placed the responsibility for these Palestinians in the hands of voluntary relief organisations. It also created an environment conducive to the development of a distinct Palestinian national identity based on the right to return and the demand for a Palestinian state. Palestinian organisations started to develop, including numerous political movements with paramilitary wings aimed at liberating Palestine through armed struggle.

The importance of the Palestinian defeat and expulsion for the Palestinian national psyche cannot be overestimated. Historical accounts, literature, art and politics from 1948 to the present day have evolved around dispossession, economic dislocation, political disenfranchisement and dispersion. Palestinian refugees, despite Arab and Israeli attempts to ignore them, played an increasingly destabilising role within their Arab host countries, within Israeli-administered territory from 1967 onwards, and in the Arab–Israeli conflict as a whole. The Palestinian refugee issue became a stumbling-block in Israel's quest for legitimacy and secure borders, as well as an obstacle to regional peace.

THE HISTORIOGRAPHICAL DEBATE

The events surrounding the first Arab–Israeli war have given rise to one of the more intense debates among historians on Israel, challenging fundamental beliefs on the creation of the state of Israel.

The historiographical debate has taken on a particularly vicious and often highly personal character, as the 'revisionist' or 'new' historians such as Avi Shlaim, Benny Morris, Ilan Pappé and Simha Flapan appear to some extent to have reinforced Arab and Palestinian claims. As pointed out in a critique of the 'new' historians, it is a group of Israelis that has given the Palestinian argument its intellectual firepower. Starting in 1987, an array of selfstyled 'new historians' has sought to debunk what it claims is a distorted 'Zionist narrative' [69]. While 'new' historians have charged 'old' historians with lacking political analysis, providing mainly personal accounts, and creating a 'popular heroic-moralistic' version of history aimed at attaining legitimacy [130], 'old' historians have accused 'new' historians of 'seeking to give academic respectability to long-standing misconceptions and prejudice' and systematically distorting 'the archival evidence to invent an Israeli history' [69].

The key issues of contention are: first, the role of the United Kingdom; secondly, Israel's victory; thirdly, the refugee problem; fourthly, Israeli–Jordanian relations; fifthly, Arab war aims; sixthly and finally, the search for peace. According to the 'new' historians, the 'old' historians maintain that British policy had been perceived generally as pro-Arab culminating in suspected British encouragement of Arab forces to invade Palestine upon the expiration of the mandate. Closer analysis of British policy, however, reveals not only that it was contradictorily anti-Arab and anti-Zionist, but above all a policy that increasingly focused on Transjordan. The Foreign Office considered the emergence of a Jewish state inevitable, but was not reconciled to the emergence of a Palestinian state which, in British eyes, was equated with a state run by Hajj Amin al-Husseini who had cast his lot with the Nazis during the Second World War [130]. British policy was clearly one of Greater Transjordan and the target of Jordan's Arab Legion in 1948 was the Palestinians and not the Jews. Transjordan's territorial claims after the war are testimony to its war aims.

The military balance in 1948 has also become a point of contention, with 'old' historians considering Israel's victory as a miraculous heroic struggle against all odds. By contrast, 'new' historians maintain that Israel won the war because its forces were essentially better trained, better motivated, better organised, and after the initial phase of the war, better armed. Rather than a miracle, the outcome of the war was a clear case of military superiority.

The Palestinian refugee problem is probably the most contentious issue as it has a direct bearing on current and future Arab–Israeli and Israeli–Palestinian relations. As one of the focal points of the Middle East peace process since 1991, it has been politically and emotionally highly charged. The underlying question is whether the Palestinians left or were expelled. 'Old' historians assert that Arab leaders called for Palestinians to leave. Arab spokesmen claim that Israel expelled the refugees. The 'new' historians have found no evidence either of Arab broadcasts or of blanket expulsion orders. 'The Palestinian refugee problem was born of war, not by design, Jewish or Arab. It was largely a by-product of Arab and Jewish fears and of the protracted, bitter fighting that characterised the first Arab–Israeli war; in smaller part, it was the deliberate creation of Jewish and Arab military commanders and politicians' [92 *p. 286*].

Israeli–Jordanian relations became the subject of controversy when 'new' historians maintained that Israel had colluded with King Abdallah of Jordan between 1947 and 1949, while 'old' historians claim that there is no evidence whatsoever of collusion. The result of this collusion was an unwritten agreement to divide Palestine following the termination of the mandate. The suggestion, of course, that Israel had Arab allies in this war, and conversely, the suggestion that King Abdallah betrayed his fellow Arabs and the Palestinians, has only added to the historiographical dispute. It also leads directly to the next issue: Transjordan's war aims and indeed those of the other invading Arab states. 'Old' historians have focused on Arab claims that their invasion of Palestine was aimed at destroying the new Jewish state. While this is supported by Arab rhetoric of that time, Arab actions, according to the 'new' historians, paint a different picture. King Abdallah's aim, for example, was not to liberate Palestine but to gain control over the territory allotted to the Arabs under the UN partition plan. King Farouk of Egypt, suspecting Transjordanian aims, joined the war of liberation to check Abdallah's ambitions. The result was a general 'land grab'. Finally, the lack of peace following the 1948 war was, in the eyes of 'old' historians, the result of Arab intransigence. 'New' historians, conversely, believe that Israel was more intransigent than the Arabs.

PEACE NEGOTIATIONS

The armistice negotiations resulted in an Israeli–Egyptian armistice on 24 February 1949, followed by an Israeli agreement with Lebanon on 23 March 1949, with Transjordan on 3 April 1949, and with Syria on 20 July 1949. Israeli politicians expected a full peace to follow soon thereafter. Official channels were established by the UN, such as the Mixed Armistice Commissions and the Lausanne Conference, semi-official contacts were made through mediators, and secret negotiations between Israel and its Arab neighbours followed the armistices. Arab–Israeli peace, however, remained elusive.

One interpretation of this period of early negotiations is that Israel wanted peace but since the Arab states were unwilling to recognise the Jewish state, there really was no one to negotiate peace with. Another reading of the situation is that Israel was intransigent and unwilling to compromise. Both reflect aspects of Israeli–Arab relations during this time, but neither is an adequate explanation for the failure to find a settlement after the 1948 war. An alternative and more comprehensive explanation can be found in state–society relations. Both Israel and the Arab states had only just moved towards independence, and consequently nation- and state-building were higher up on the list of priorities than peace. Both had a strong society and a comparatively weak state, and were still in the process of construction and legitimisation.

The defeat in the 1948 war led to instability in the Arab states as a result of domestic challenges to the leadership which had lost the war, rivalry between the Arab states in pursuit of regional hegemony, the rise of Arab nationalism, and an emerging tendency towards more revolutionary ideologies. The extent of instability becomes clear when looking at the years between the first Arab–Israeli war and the 1956 Suez war. Egypt's monarchy was overthrown in the 1952 Free Officers coup. King Abdallah of Jordan was assassinated in 1951, succeeded by his eldest son Talal who reigned until May 1953 when he was deposed and succeeded by Hussein. In 1951 Lebanon's Prime Minister Riad as-Sulh was assassinated, and in 1952 President Bishara al-Khoury was deposed in a bloodless coup and replaced by Camille Chamoun. In Syria, General Husni Zaim staged a military coup in May 1949. He was overthrown a few months later by Sami al-Hinnawi, who in turn was deposed by another coup in December 1949 by Adib Shishakli. In 1954 Shishakli was overthrown and forced to flee. Hashem al-Atassi then held the presidency until 1955 when he was replaced by Shukri al-Kuwatli. In comparison, Israel was more stable. That did not, however, mean that there was no tension within the decision-making elite. In fact, a major rift was emerging between Prime Minister David Ben Gurion and Foreign Minister Moshe Sharett over the direction of Israel's foreign and defence policy. Ultimately, Ben Gurion's hardline security-driven policy – as opposed to Sharett's 'softer' diplomatic approach – won the upper hand in 1955.

In light of these instabilities, tensions and leadership challenges, it is not surprising that major Arab–Israeli diplomatic initiatives did not result in peace [110]. Immediately following the 1948 war, Israel initiated a diplomatic offensive to start secretly negotiating with Jordan.

Jordan was seen as the Arab state most likely to sign peace with Israel based on the Zionist–Jordanian alliance during the war. Contacts between Israeli leaders and King Abdallah had always been amicable and, from an Israeli perspective, it was therefore not surprising that in February 1950 a non-belligerence agreement between the two was concluded. Jordan, however, never ratified this agreement. The main stumbling-block in the search for peace was King Abdallah's insistence on territorial concessions. Israel had only just acquired the territory it needed to achieve territorial contiguity and defensible borders. The notion of land for peace was unacceptable from an Israeli perspective. Territorial concessions were also the main point of contention in Israel's secret negotiations with Syria and Egypt. Syria demanded half of the Sea of Galilee, and Egypt wanted parts of the Negev desert in return for full peace.

One final observation should be made at this point. Both official diplomatic initiatives and secret negotiations reveal that while attempts were being made to resolve the dispute between Israel and the Arab states, the Palestinian dimension had been completely marginalised. In fact, it could be said that Israel used contacts with its Arab neighbours to by-pass the Palestinians, while Arab leaders, in turn, only played the Palestinian card to consolidate their own political position domestically and regionally. Indeed, Jordan's annexation of the West Bank in April 1950 made it very clear that there was little Arab support for a separate Palestinian state.

Conflicting expectations, aims and perceptions as well as intransigence on both sides led to discord in the early Arab–Israeli negotiations. The aims of the Arab states were the acquisition of territory and the repatriation of Palestinian refugees. Israel's aims were recognition and peace without giving up territory. At the same time the weakness of state and government and the strength of society, discouraged risk-taking by political representatives and shifted the political agenda towards state consolidation. Despite perceptions that peace would be achieved in due time after the armistice agreements, the right conditions for conflict-resolution simply did not exist. The Arab states might have lost the war, but they were not defeated to such an extent that they were 'forced' to make peace at all costs. Israel, conversely, while desiring peace and recognition, was also not ready to make territorial concessions. International mediation, which could have brought the parties in the conflict closer to a settlement, was indecisive. The great powers were far from impartial brokers, being preoccupied with the emerging Cold War. There were no incentives or, indeed, benefits for Arab–Israeli recognition and acceptance of each other. The lack of 'stateness' did not provide leaders and diplomats with sufficient security and stability to pursue peace. In short, the so-called ripe moment had not come.

3   THE 1956 SUEZ–SINAI CAMPAIGN

The inconclusive outcome of the first Arab–Israeli war and the inability to conclude a peace agreement led both Israel and its Arab neighbours to believe that ultimately there was going to be a second round. Israeli diplomats had been unsuccessful in attaining the recognition and international legitimacy Israel desired, and Israel's army was unable to fully secure its borders. The Arab regimes, in turn, were suffering from domestic challenges as well as regional insecurity. Arab–Israeli tensions were further exacerbated by the unresolved issue of Palestinian refugees, and influenced by the emerging Cold War in the Middle East. The latter has set in motion the on-going debate over whether the Cold War was imposed upon the region by the superpowers, or whether it was imported by regional actors for their own ends.

THE 1952 EGYPTIAN COUP

On 23 July 1952 Egypt's monarchy was overthrown by the Free Officers whose six-point charter called for 'ousting the king, ending colonialism, strengthening the army, social equality, economic development and free education for all' [23 p. 44]. Egyptian journalist and diplomat Mohamed Heikal describes the reasons for the coup as follows:

> Discontent in the armed forces had been smouldering for a long time. At the beginning of 1946 there had been massive demonstrations by students and workers in Cairo, Alexandria, and other towns, involving loss of life. Then had come the defeats and humiliations of the Palestine war. Two prime ministers had been assassinated, as had been Hassan al-Banna, the Supreme Guide of the Moslem Brotherhood, the latter by members of the special police. All this continuing unrest and frustration increased the contempt felt by the armed forces for their nominal head, King Farouk. [63 p. 28]

Reasons for the revolution further included the old regime's association with the colonial powers as well as its inability during the 1948 war adequately to supply the Egyptian army with arms in order to defeat Israel. After the Free Officers coup, King Farouk went into exile while Egypt under the leadership of President and Prime Minister Mohammed Naguib and his deputy Gamal Abdel Nasser instituted far-reaching socio-economic reforms. Nasser replaced Naguib in October 1954, and through his policies of non-alignment, Arab unity and Arab socialism propelled Egypt into a position of leadership in the Middle East and the Third World.

Both Israel and the West initially regarded the new Egyptian government with favour. It was seen as more reasonable than the *Wafd** nationalists had been. Nasser appeared to be a moderate leader with vision, idealism and honour. The new regime was welcomed by the United States in particular, which had been looking for popular pro-Western leaders [47]. American aid, numerous invitations to send Egyptians on training missions and a strong US diplomatic presence marked this honeymoon period [63]. Israel, too, saw the change of government as a new opportunity for settlement. 'The Israelis were hopeful of a breakthrough. Much of their optimism centred on one man, Gamal Abdel Nasser ... he had participated in the cease-fire talks with Israel in 1949 and had expressed a desire to resolve the conflict' [98 *p. 14*]. In fact, intense secret Israeli–Egyptian diplomatic efforts were initiated and pursued until 1956. The perceptions of Nasser changed, however, when he refused to join the Baghdad Pact and negotiated the Czech arms deal in 1955. Hopes for peace gave way to distrust, animosity, and finally war.

ISRAELI–EGYPTIAN TENSIONS

The 1949 armistice agreement did not result in a stable border situation. Indeed, Israeli historian Benny Morris asserts that 'even before the ink on the armistice agreements was dry, there arose in the Arab capitals a clamour for an avenging second round' [94 *p. 9*]. This second round was aimed at redeeming the Palestinians and defeating Israel. 'Second round thinking', however, was also evident in Israel where it was seen as a way to establish a more defensible border as well as achieve territorial expansion.

The permeability of Israel's border exacerbated tensions. Palestinians infiltrated Israel from their camps in the Gaza Strip, as well as from Jordan and Syria. The motivations for crossing into Israel ranged from attempts to reunify families, harvest fields and orchards left behind, regain property, and trade, to sabotaging Israel's infrastructure and attacking civilian and military targets. As the Palestinians were becoming more organised in the mid-1950s, paramilitary or *fedayeen** raids on Israel became more frequent and successful. In 1950, 19 Israeli civilians were killed and 31 wounded; in 1951, 48 were killed and 49 wounded; in 1952, 42 were killed and 56 wounded; in 1953, 44 were killed and 66 wounded; in 1954, 33 were killed and 77 wounded; in 1955, 24 were killed and 69 wounded; and in 1956, 54 were killed and 129 wounded [94 *p. 98*]. In the face of these figures, Israeli decision-makers opted for a policy of retaliation, shoot-to-kill orders, mining of border areas, and expulsion operations. The first major retaliatory strike was the Qibya raid on 14 October 1953 which was ordered by Ben Gurion in retaliation for an attack on the settlement of Yehud, during which an Israeli mother and her two children were killed [98]. The perpetrators' tracks led to the Jordanian border. The village of Qibya had regularly appeared in Israeli intelligence reports as a base for infiltrators, and thus became the target for Israeli retaliatory action aimed at 'blowing up houses and hitting the inhabitants' [94]. Forty-five houses were destroyed and 69 people killed, half of them women and children [47].

Egyptian–Israeli relations were also deteriorating over border clashes and infiltrations. Egyptian efforts to curb infiltration along the Gaza Strip were unsuccessful. By mid-1953 Israeli intelligence asserted that Egyptians were employing minelayers and saboteurs, using Bedouin as guides [94]. Israel accused the Egyptian authorities of instigating the infiltrations. Closer analysis of Egyptian policy, however, suggests that Egyptian support for saboteurs only started after the 1955 Gaza raid.

Tensions were further exacerbated in July 1954, when a group of Israeli agents in collaboration with Egyptian Jews tried to sabotage British and American property in Egypt in order to create discord between the Egyptian government and the West and to persuade the British that their military presence was still needed [136]. British withdrawal from the Suez Canal Zone would effectively remove the buffer between Egypt and Israel and, worse still, Egypt would become eligible for US military aid [23 *p. 51*]. The Israeli operation failed when the saboteurs were apprehended, resulting in Israeli–Egyptian tension as well as jeopardising the secret talks in Paris. The so-called Lavon affair, as it came to be known, provided Ben Gurion with the opportunity to manoeuvre himself back into the premiership. With him the activist approach to foreign and defence policy returned in full force.

In February 1955 an Egyptian intelligence-gathering squad entered Israel and killed an Israeli cyclist near Rehovot. In retaliation, Israel launched the Gaza raid on 28 February, killing 38 Egyptian soldiers. Retrospectively, it has often been asserted that this particular infiltration only provided Israel with the 'pretext for an operation designed to show Israel's military power both to the West and a nervous public opinion' [47 *p. 64*]. Nasser considered the Gaza raid to be the turning point in Israeli–Egyptian relations and maintained that Israeli action was the primary reason for Egypt turning to the Soviet bloc in search for arms. Indeed, Egyptian accounts of the raid describe it as 'an action of unprovoked aggression carried out with deliberate brutality'. The raid was intended as a message from Ben Gurion to Nasser, and Nasser understood the message [59 *p. 66*].

Nasser's response was the Czech arms deal and the closure of the Straits of Tiran in 1955, which in the eyes of Israel changed the regional balance to a much less favourable one. The deal provided Egypt with 100 self-propelled guns, 200 armoured personnel carriers, 300 tanks, 200 MiG 15 jets and 50 Ilyushin-28 bombers [47 *p. 66*]. In an attempt to redress the situation, Israel courted French military aid, resulting in the supply of 12 Mystère IV fighters in April 1956, followed by another 72 Mystères, 120 AMX light tanks and 40 Super Sherman tanks.

The Czech arms deal also set in motion Israeli deliberations on a pre-emptive war. Ben Gurion's reaction to the deal was recorded in Moshe Sharett's diary as follows: 'If they really get MiGs – I will be for bombing them!' [126], and Moshe Dayan in his diary of the Sinai campaign stated that 'if the Arab states, led by the ruler of Egypt, had not pursued a policy of increasing enmity towards her, Israel would not have resorted to arms' [33 *p. 11*]. Dayan's statement is interesting in that it obscures a crucial debate taking place in the Israeli decision-making elite which has carried over into the historiography of the conflict. At the heart of both debates is the issue of Israeli interventionism. In short, to what extent was Israeli policy only reactive?

THE ISRAELI FOREIGN AND DEFENCE POLICY DEBATE

In the years immediately following the establishment of the state, Israel firmly established itself regionally and internationally. The state successfully absorbed Jewish refugees from Europe and embarked upon the more long-term integration of Jewish immigrants from Asia and North Africa. The priority of the fledgling state, however, remained its security, placing a large burden on society, politics and the economy. It also triggered an intense debate between the Israeli Prime Minister and Defence Minister David Ben Gurion and Foreign Minister Moshe Sharett.

Ben Gurion's approach to foreign policy was based on large-scale intervention and resorting to covert operations in order to inject disunity into the enemy camp. It was aimed at keeping the Arabs off-balance and retarding their efforts to modernise their military [130]. At the core of Ben Gurion's activism was the belief that the Arabs were incapable of accepting peaceful co-existence. Israel's security, therefore, took precedence. It was within this context that Ben Gurion advocated retaliation, the use of force, and pre-emptive war. His main challenger within the Israeli decision-making elite was Sharett, who advocated a much more cautious approach. Long-range implications were the focus of this view. With peace as the ultimate goal for the region, Sharett argued that Arab disunity was against Israel's interests as Arab consensus was needed in furthering the cause of peace [124].

Simplistically, it was a debate between 'hawks' and 'doves', which was enforced by tensions in the personal relationship between Ben Gurion and Sharett, who had shared the governance of the Jewish state project since the 1930s. 'Sharett admired and respected Ben Gurion – but also felt overawed, overshadowed, and occasionally, jealous. Ben Gurion, for his part, while respecting Sharett's analytical and diplomatic skills, and his mastery of languages, was envious of Sharett's man-of-the-world sociability and *savoir-faire*. People liked and respected Sharett; they "merely" admired Ben Gurion and stood in awe of him' [94 p. 230].

Ultimately, Ben Gurion's activist approach prevailed because of the strong involvement of the security sphere and defence establishment in decision-making. Sharett's unsuccessful attempt at the premiership followed by the Sinai Campaign settled the debate in Ben Gurion's favour.

The importance of this debate emerges when returning to the Czech arms deal from a historiographical perspective. The conventional view sees the Sinai Campaign as the result of the influx of Soviet arms and the blockade of the Straits of Tiran. This view has been challenged by historians such as Motti Golani who claims that 'on the contrary, the arms deal temporarily blocked Israel's efforts to launch a war' [53 p. 804]. This implies that war was on the cards much earlier, setting the parameters of the debate: When did Israel plan to go to war? And was the war the result of a broader interventionist policy?

BRITISH–FRENCH–ISRAELI COLLABORATION

The 1956 Suez–Sinai war consisted of two separate military operations, one Anglo-French and one Israeli, with the overarching aim to
depose Nasser. It was the result of a convergence of interests and sim-
ilar perceptions of Nasser rather than a long-standing strategic relationship. Indeed, Israeli–British relations had been rocky as Israeli
interests prior to 1956 had often been diametrically opposed to those
of the UK [82]. France and Israel, on the other hand, had already
developed a cordial relationship with the premiership of Pierre
Mendes-France, which was strengthened by Egyptian–French tensions
over the Algerian war. Ben Gurion saw Nasser as a direct threat to
Israel while France considered Egypt to be the main support to Algerian
nationalists fighting for their independence from France. As a result
of their mutual antagonism, Israel was able to acquire French war
planes as well as assistance in developing its first nuclear reactor
[104].

In spring 1956 French decision-makers came to the conclusion that
the only way to control the Algerian revolution was to overthrow
Nasser. Plans for an assault on Egypt were deliberated at length. The
nationalisation of the Suez Canal on 26 July 1956 made French–
Egyptian collision almost inevitable. Moreover, France was no longer
isolated in its opposition to Nasser, but had been joined by Britain
and Israel. French shuttle diplomacy between the British and Israelis in
September and October resulted in the sought-after tripartite alliance.

Britain's perception of Nasser did not differ much from that of the
French. British influence in the Middle East had been in decline since
1945 and the British share of oil production had decreased from 49
per cent to 14 per cent [99 *p. 154*]. The Suez Canal consequently
became the major focal point of, and Egypt the main obstacle to, British
Middle East policy. In addition, Nasser's pursuit of neutralism had
stood in the way of Anglo-American attempts to create a Middle East
defence organisation along the lines of NATO*, and Nasser's determination to reform and modernise Egypt not only economically but
also militarily provided the Soviet Union with an entry point. Moreover, Nasser was able to mobilise support against the remaining conservative Arab regimes in the Middle East, which were Britain's traditional allies, as well as against the British presence in Africa. The
conclusion was simple: Nasser had to go.

British perceptions of the Egyptian problem were two-fold. First,
Egypt's refusal to join the Baghdad Pact followed by the Czech arms
deal was seen as a sign that Egypt was coming increasingly under
Soviet influence [*Doc. 8*]. Secondly, the nationalisation of the Suez

Canal not only deprived Britain of its profits but was also perceived as a political and even military challenge. Much of British shipping, especially oil tankers, had to pass through the canal. The British decision underlying military action can to some extent also be traced back to the failure of its appeasement policy in Europe.

The key to understanding Nasser's decisions, in comparison, can be found in his policy of neutralism and his assumption that military action following the nationalisation of the Suez Canal would not necessarily follow. The period of maximum danger, according to Nasser, was the first few days. Then international opinion would eliminate this risk [59]. After all, when the Anglo–Iranian Oil Company was nationalised on 1 May 1951, Britain 'only' imposed sanctions while the United States even supported it whole heartedly. Moreover, Nasser needed to nationalise the Canal in order to finance the Aswan Dam, a project of great prestige and personal legitimacy which the United States had stopped funding in July 1956 in an attempt to humiliate and control Nasser.

The nationalisation of the Suez Canal on 26 July 1956 in order to obtain the financing for the Aswan Dam provided the *casus belli* for Anglo-French decision-makers, in the way that the Czech arms deal and the complete sealing of the Straits of Tiran in September 1955 had provided the *casus belli* for Israel. Britain and France refused to recognise Egypt's sovereignty over the canal. As early as 29 July 1956 France started to consider military co-operation with Israel against Egypt. While there were no obstacles in the relations between France and Israel, British–Israeli relations were strained as the result of the British–Jordanian defence arrangement. Jordanian–Israeli border tensions were high and the instability in the Hashemite Kingdom of Jordan prompted the British to suggest moving Iraqi troops into Jordan during the forthcoming parliamentary elections. Israel saw this as a direct threat, as Iraq was the only state not to have signed the 1949 armistice. In light of the tripartite plans against Nasser, Israeli decision-makers found Britain's attitude incomprehensible. Only on 16 October at a meeting in Paris was the situation finally resolved. Britain agreed to Israel's participation in the Suez war and called off its Jordanian plans.

The plan [*Doc. 9*], which has been described as 'ill-conceived both in organisation and purpose' [47], called for Israel to seize the Suez Canal. Britain and France would then ask Egypt and Israel to withdraw from the canal. Counting upon Egypt's refusal to do so, Anglo-French troops would be forced to intervene in order to protect the canal. Ben Gurion wanted to delay the campaign until after the US presidential election on 6 November in order to secure American backing. Yet Dayan set the invasion date for 29 October. In his diary Dayan describes the situation with the USA as 'complicated, and not at all agreeable'.

> Israel, wishing and needing to maintain close ties of friendship with the US, finds herself in the difficult position of having to keep from her – and even be evasive about – her real intentions. ... The US is adamantly opposed to any military action on the part of Israel, yet she does not – perhaps she cannot – prevent anti-Israel action on the part of the Arabs. Moreover, the US consistently refuses to grant or sell us arms, thereby exposing us to aggression by the Arabs who have open access to arms from the Soviet bloc. [33 *p. 74*]

On 30 October, Israeli troops reached the canal. Britain and France issued an ultimatum for both Israeli and Egyptian forces to withdraw from the area. Nasser, as predicted, rejected the ultimatum and thereby 'provoked' the British and French bombing of Egyptian airfields on 31 October. For the next two days 200 British and French fighter-bombers destroyed economic targets in Egypt as well as Egypt's air-force. British and French paratroops subsequently invaded, only to be forced to halt their military operation as a result of US pressure.

Ironically, despite US opposition to the tripartite attack on Egypt, the American analysis of Nasser was not necessarily different from that of Britain, France and Israel. The lack of American support for an Anglo-French military operation was not based on the belief that Nasser should remain in power, but to a large degree on US President Dwight D. Eisenhower's election campaign. The use of force had to be delayed until its successful conclusion. Consequently it is not surprising that Eisenhower, hearing of the Israeli attack while on a campaign trip to Florida, felt deceived. He told US Secretary of State John Foster Dulles to 'tell them goddam it, we are going to apply sanctions, we are going to the United Nations, we are going to do everything that there is to stop this thing' [40 *p. 73*]. Eisenhower erroneously suspected that Ben Gurion had deliberately chosen the timing in order to assure Israel of US approval through pressure from the Jewish lobby. He felt even further betrayed when Britain and France joined in the Suez war.

Israel was condemned for aggression, economic sanctions were applied, and the severing of US–Israeli relations was threatened should Israel decide to stay in the Sinai. On 2 November 1956 the UN General Assembly approved a US-sponsored resolution for an immediate cease-fire and withdrawal of all forces from Egyptian territory. Israel, under severe US pressure, was forced to accept the cease-fire, leaving Britain and France in a difficult situation. Britain and France were still in the midst of their invasion and had not seized control of the canal. Financial pressure brought to bear on Britain finally forced Anthony Eden to give in to mounting Cabinet pressure and agree to a cease-fire as well, and Guy Mollet reluctantly went along.

The American intervention to halt the joint British–French–Israeli operation can be explained, firstly, by the belief that a full-scale war would result in Soviet intervention in the Middle East. US Secretary of State John Foster Dulles, for example, saw the Suez Canal as the crucial link for oil supplies to NATO, and an opportunity for the Soviet Union to restrict the canal would weaken Western European resistance to communism [6]. The second factor was the US policy of even-handedness in the Arab–Israeli conflict, which was motivated by oil interests as well as preventing an arms race. The third element was Eisenhower's 1956 election campaign on a peace platform. And fourthly, the fact that the United States had condemned Soviet intervention in Hungary not only made it difficult to support intervention in Egypt, but the latter also diverted attention from Soviet action. The underlying US mistrust of Soviet motives became clear on 1 November, when Eisenhower and Dulles at a National Security Council* meeting stated that 'if we were not now prepared to assert our leadership in this cause, leadership would certainly be seized by the Soviet Union' [14 *p. 273*]. Indeed, the convergence of the crisis in the Middle East and events in Hungary created an atmosphere in which the fear of a possible US–Soviet nuclear confrontation spread [6].

THE RESULTS OF THE WAR

The war ended in a resounding military defeat for Nasser. Yet from a regional post-war perspective, Nasser clearly emerged on the winning side. Dismissing Israel's Sinai campaign as non-existent, he was hailed as the only Arab leader able to challenge the West and to expel the British and French imperialist forces as well as Israel from Egyptian territory. From this position Nasser expanded his regional influence and established Egypt's leadership of the Arab world. He had been able to hold on to the Suez Canal. During the war he had also been able to nationalise the remaining British and French holdings, providing funds for the Aswan Dam and the modernisation of Egypt. He had even acquired an international army, UNEF*, to protect Egypt from Israeli retaliatory policy.

Israel, too had gained from the war, despite its failure to depose Nasser. UNEF guaranteed freedom of shipping in the Gulf of Aqaba, providing Israel with a Red Sea port. UNEF also provided some limited control over the *fedayeen* infiltrations. Most importantly, however, Israel's military reputation had been further enhanced. The speed with which Israeli troops were able to advance on the Suez Canal elevated Israel's status to that of regional superpower. It could even be argued that the Sinai campaign was able to deter a further Arab–Israeli war and thus provide Israel with the space to complete its nation-building and state-building.

France and Britain are generally considered to be the losers of the war. Egypt remained in total control of the canal, and the perception that Nasser had successfully challenged the former colonial powers led to a further decline of British and French influence in the Middle East as well as in Africa and South-East Asia. Neither Britain nor France was able to counter the damage to an already declining diplomatic position. The United States and the Soviet Union, in comparison, were able to step into this vacuum and emerged as the two 'new' foreign powers in the Middle East. As a result the Arab–Israeli conflict had become an arena for the Cold War. In addition, it raised a further point of scholarly contention: the question to what extent the Cold War had been imposed upon the region by the United States and the Soviet Union – and to what extent the Cold War was imported into the region and manipulated by regional leaders for their own ends [51; 118].

4 THE 1967 SIX DAY WAR

The Six Day War was the third Arab–Israeli war in less than two decades. It was triggered by a growing intensity in attacks on Israel as well as increasing Israeli retaliation against its Arab neighbours in late 1966 and early 1967. It was a war that took many in the international community by surprise, a confrontation that neither Israel, Egypt, Syria and Jordan, nor the United States and the Soviet Union claim to have wanted. Yet the decline into confrontation seemed almost inevitable from 1966 onwards. Israel's perception of vulnerability; hostile Israeli, Egyptian and Syrian rhetoric; continuing border tensions; and finally Egyptian troop movements to the Sinai, the withdrawal of UNEF, and the closing of the Straits of Tiran, left little room for diplomatic manoeuvring. It has, however, left room for quite an amount of speculation in the search for an explanation.

In Israeli historiography the blame for the war clearly rests with Nasser who, by closing the Straits of Tiran, left Israel with no alternative but to fight. Another version advanced in the historiographical debate is that Nasser did not intend to go to war. His threats were not aimed at Israel but at his fellow Arabs to whom he wished to prove that he was still the champion of pan-Arabism. Accordingly, it was misplaced Israeli reaction that led to war. A third explanation of events is embodied in the so-called 'accident' theory, which lays the blame for the conflict on regional dynamics as a whole rather than one particular player. The Six Day War was the result of Egyptian–Israeli brinkmanship that went over the brink. Neither wanted war, but both had to keep up with the other's hostile rhetoric. The final historiographical contender to be mentioned here, is the argument that the war was really the result of US–Soviet manipulation of regional powers, seeing the Cold War as the defining context.

THE CREATION OF THE PALESTINE LIBERATION ORGANISATION

The 1956 Suez crisis had once again shown the focus of Arab leaders to be on their own foreign and domestic problems rather than on the conviction to liberate Palestine. The Arab world and the international community seemed to have forgotten about the plight of the Palestinian refugees. It was this realisation that led to a Palestinian political and military revival. Building on earlier underground nationalist groups, Fatah* was formed in 1957 in Kuwait, and renewed Palestinian resistance was organised under the leadership of Yasser Arafat, Khalil Wazir and Salah Khalaf.

In an attempt to control the Palestinian *fedayeen* and to prevent their actions from completely destabilising the region, Nasser established the Palestine Liberation Organisation (PLO)* in January 1964 at an Arab summit meeting in Cairo. This new Palestinian organisation also provided Nasser with leadership credentials in his regional rivalry with Syria and Iraq. Thus it is not surprising that the PLO soon became the object of an inter-Arab struggle for influence between Egypt, Syria and Iraq, as well as an Arab–Palestinian struggle for control.

From its establishment onwards the PLO served as an umbrella for all Palestinian resistance groups, providing political and military co-ordination when needed, but essentially leaving individual groups free to act. Its main political institution was the Palestine National Council (PNC)*, which met for the first time in East Jerusalem in May 1964 to draft its Covenant [*Doc. 10*]. The Covenant was a political manifesto and a constitution at the same time, laying claim to Palestine as a future state and designating armed struggle as the means to this end. During its first few years of existence the PNC comprised only 100 members, but as the PLO expanded and embarked upon a clear path of emancipation from the Arab states, PNC membership increased to 600. Real power, however, lay with the small Executive Committee, which consisted of the top PLO leadership.

The first head of the PLO was Palestinian lawyer Ahmad al-Shukayri, who had served as Saudi Arabia's UN representative and was personally chosen by Nasser. Indeed, up until 1967 the PLO remained very much under Arab and particularly Egyptian control. Units of its official army, the Palestine Liberation Army (PLA)* were trained and to some extent integrated into the various Arab armies. Yet Arab control was never all-pervasive and soon after 1964 independent Palestinian *fedayeen* operations against Israel started to increase again, reinforcing Israel's feeling of vulnerability.

ON THE BRINK OF WAR

The Six Day War was the result of political developments, which began with the change of government in Syria on 23 February 1966. The rise to power of militant Ba'thists resulted in increasingly hostile rhetoric at a time when already bad Syrian–Israeli border relations were deteriorating. The road to conflict, however, was not really embarked upon until August 1966, when Israel and Syria clashed in a fierce battle in the area of the Sea of Galilee [136]. This was followed in November by Egypt signing a mutual defence pact with Syria. The pact boosted Syria's confidence but, at the same time, increased Israel's threat perception. Syrian and Egyptian moves were compounded by continued *fedayeen* operations against Israel from Jordan. In light of this triple threat, Israeli decision-makers adopted a more hard-line security response. On 13 November, Israel launched its most extensive operation since the Sinai Campaign when the IDF raided the West Bank villages of as-Samu, Jimba and Khirbet Karkay. Three Jordanian civilians and fifteen Arab Legion soldiers were killed, while another 54 civilians and military personnel were wounded. A clinic, a school and 140 houses were damaged. Thus it is not surprising that by the end of the year the region was once again, on the brink of war.

The tensions continued through the first half of 1967. In April, Israel and Syria engaged in an airbattle over Syria, in which Syria lost six MiGs. A future all–out military confrontation seemed almost unavoidable. The final factor to set the ball rolling was a Soviet intelligence report. On 13 May, Soviet President Nikolai Podgorny told Nasser's aide Anwar Sadat, who was on a visit to Moscow, that Israeli troops had mobilised and intended to invade Syria [20]. With this report Soviet intelligence confirmed earlier reports from Syria. As Nasser was bound by the mutual defence pact, he decided to act immediately, despite the fact that Israel, as confirmed by a UN inspection team, had not mobilised or deployed [136]. The false Soviet intelligence report has ever since been the subject of intense speculation. One possible motivation for planting this information is that the Soviet Union wanted to take pressure off Syria [47], believing that both Israel and the Arabs would stop short of war [20]. Another explanation is that it was simply an inaccurate and poorly evaluated report. A third possibility is that the Soviet Union was deliberately misled by Israel, either to intimidate Syria, or to draw Egypt into the fight. The fourth possibility is that the Soviet Union wanted a war [24]. This explanation is supported by Evgeny Pyrlin, Head of the Egypt Department of the Soviet Foreign Ministry at that time, who claims that Soviet decision-makers believed 'that even if the war was not won by our side – the Egyptians – a war would be to our political advantage because the Egyptians would have demonstrated their ability to fight with our weapons and with our military and political support' [23 *p. 65*]. A final explanation is based on a Cold War globalist perspective, according to which, the Soviet Union deliberately issued false information in order to create another conflict for the United States so as to weaken the American position in Vietnam.

Regardless of Soviet motives, Nasser reacted swiftly. On 14 May, Egyptian troops moved into the Sinai. It has been claimed that this move was purely a measure of deterrence aimed at Israel as well as assuring Syria. 'Dangerous though it seemed, this troop deployment did not signal that war was imminent' [47]. Nasser's request for the partial withdrawal of UNEF confirms this to a degree. UN Secretary-General U Thant's insistence on either 'no withdrawal or complete withdrawal' instead left the Egyptian–Israeli border without a buffer. Nasser, who had been taunted by rival Arab leaders that he was hiding behind the UN, had no choice but to opt for complete withdrawal. Yet the specific Egyptian request for UNEF to withdraw from Sharm al-Sheikh, from where Egypt could close the Straits of Tiran to Israeli shipping, could also be interpreted as a deliberate act of war – and indeed was by Israel.

Following the withdrawal of UNEF from Sinai, U Thant urged Israel to accept UN troops on its side of the frontier in order to maintain a buffer [136]. As such a move did not prevent Egypt from closing the Straits of Tiran, the offer was rejected. On 22 May, Nasser proceeded to close the Straits, later claiming that he had no choice if he wanted to return 'things to what they were in 1956' [78]. Interestingly, he did not believe that his action would lead to war. Rather, he would gain a political victory and deflect Arab criticism [131]. As Egyptian Minister of War Shams Badran recalls: 'the Arab countries kept on saying that we were allowing Israeli ships to go through Eilat, and that Eilat was the main port for Israeli exports. The attack against us – in Jordanian and Saudi propaganda – was fierce, and showed us that we had to do something to stop the Israeli ships going through the Straits' [23 *p. 68*]. Israeli decision-makers, having stated their position repeatedly since 1956, regarded this act as a clear *casus belli*. Indeed, from the Israeli perspective, Egypt's aggressive intent was confirmed when Jordan joined the general mobilisation on 21 May, followed by the signing of a mutual defence agreement with Egypt on 30 May. By that point, Israel too had started to mobilise with the overall result of 80,000 Egyptian troops and 900 tanks, 300

Syrian tanks, 300 Jordanian tanks, and some 250,000 Israeli troops, 1,093 tanks and 203 planes ready for action. War seemed inevitable.

All through May, Israeli public anxiety and military frustration increased while diplomats tried to diffuse the crisis. Israeli attempts to negotiate the opening of the Straits with Egyptian Vice-President Zakariya Muhieddin in Washington on 3 June failed, against the backdrop of increasingly hostile rhetoric from all belligerents. The Israeli public demanded action, and Israeli Prime Minister Levi Eshkol more and more felt the need to assert himself *vis-à-vis* Ben Gurion's constant criticism from the comfort of retirement. As a result, on 4 June, Israel's national unity government was established. Eshkol was forced to hand over the defence portfolio to Moshe Dayan, who then took the decision to go to war. It was clear that if Israel did not strike first, the Arabs would.

THE SIX DAY WAR

On 5 June 1967 Israel launched its pre-emptive strike. The Israeli air-force destroyed 304 Egyptian, 53 Syrian and 28 Jordanian aircraft, mostly on the ground [20 *p. 222–3*]. The IDF crossed into the Sinai and into the West Bank. Syria, Jordan and Egypt counter-attacked the same day. The three Arab states became embroiled in a land battle with the Jewish state, which continued until 10 June. However, without air cover for troops and tanks, the Arab forces were easy prey. The war with Egypt ended when Israeli forces occupied Sharm al-Sheikh and reached the Suez Canal. Having lost 2,000 soldiers in the fighting with Israel and another 10,000 in the retreat, Egypt had no choice but to agree to a cease-fire on 8 June. Jordan's position was no better. King Hussein recalled his troops coming back in small groups, deprived of air cover and defeated. 'I saw all the years I had spent since 1953 trying to build up the country and army, all the pride, all the hopes, destroyed' [23 *p. 91*]. The battle on the West Bank ended when Israel captured East Jerusalem on 7 June and troops moved to the Jordan River before King Hussein agreed to the cease-fire later in the day. Syrian–Israeli fighting did not even start until 9 June. Indeed, Israel only attacked Syria once Jordan and Egypt had been defeated. 'Shortly after midnight on the ninth, Syria, which had contributed so much to the crisis and nothing to the conflict' also agreed to a cease-fire [131].

The war left Israel in control of Jordan's West Bank, Egypt's Sinai peninsula and the Gaza Strip, and Syria's Golan Heights [*Map 2*]. Israel's air superiority was the most important factor in Israel's victory,

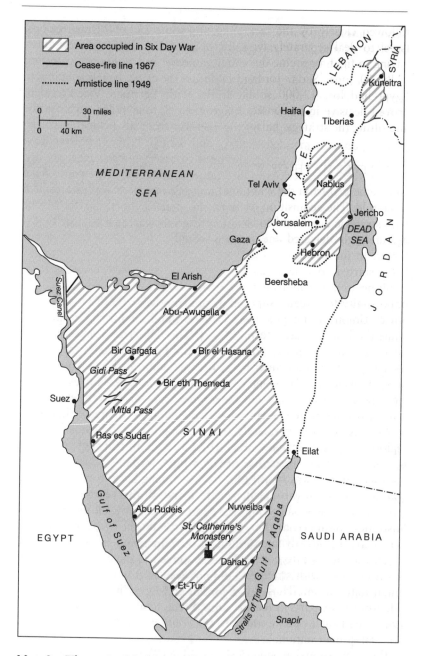

Map 2   The revised borders after the Six Day War

followed closely by the lack of Arab co-ordination which enabled Israel to deal separately with Egypt, Jordan and Syria rather than having to fight a genuine three-frontal war.

By 10 June, Syria, Jordan and Egypt had agreed to cease-fires. Egypt had lost 12,000 soldiers, Israel 766. As in 1948, this war proved decisive in its consequences, both increasing Israel's territory and tilting the strategic balance unequivocally in Israel's favour.

THE AFTERMATH OF WAR

Israel emerged from the war victorious and had increased its territory three-fold. The acquisition of this additional territory provided Israel with strategic depth and consequently more security. Nasser had been resoundingly defeated and was no longer considered to be the main threat. In the wake of his demise, the more radical Ba'thi regime in Syria started to emerge as Israel's main regional rival, ultimately resulting in a Syrian–Israeli arms race which, in turn, provided the opportunity for greater superpower involvement. The prestige of the Soviet Union, as Egypt's and Syria's ally, had also been damaged, while the United States started to see Israel as a valuable asset in the region through which to counter Soviet influence [144]. US support for Israel was based primarily on Israel's military strength and reliability as well as Israel's opposition to the radical Arab states which were perceived as Soviet clients. Added to this was an element of affinity derived from shared moral and political standards [83].

As a result of the war, Israel emerged as the dominant power in the region. The Arab regimes, despite proclaiming a victory, had been humiliated, which triggered another period of domestic challenges and instability. Egypt was forced to abandon its involvement in the Yemen war, and Nasser saw his claim to leadership of the Arab world greatly reduced. In 1968 Syria had another military coup, while Egyptian–Israeli hostilities continued as the War of Attrition 1968–69. With the Six Day War, regional dynamics had also changed. Pan-Arabism started to decline and had to compete not only with the emergence of pan-Islam but also with strengthened local nationalisms including Palestinian nationalism. Thus, by discrediting Nasser and 'ejecting Arab rule from those parts of mandatory Palestine which had been saved in 1948', the Israeli victory contributed to the re-focusing on particularistic Palestinian nationalism as well as placing the Palestinians back on the international agenda [64].

The Six Day War also provided the international community once again with the opportunity to attempt the conclusion of a regional settlement. Disagreement between the United States and the Soviet Union, however, revealed an almost unbridgeable gap. In light of this superpower stalemate, the diplomatic focus shifted to the United Nations. The result of numerous sessions was UN Security Council Resolution 242. It emphasised 'the inadmissibility of the acquisition of territory by war' and acknowledged 'the sovereignty, territorial integrity and political independence of every state in the area and their right to live in peace within secure and recognised boundaries free from acts of force' [*Doc. 11*]. The resolution also called for a just and lasting peace based on the Israeli withdrawal from territories occupied during the war, and reaffirmed the necessity of a 'just settlement of the refugee problem'.

Resolution 242 embodied all those key elements which had to be addressed for conflict resolution: recognition, inadmissibility of acquiring territory by war, freedom from acts of force, peace, and the Palestinian refugee problem. These, however, were not seized upon until the Madrid peace process some 25 years later. In the meantime, the Arabs insisted that 242 called for Israeli withdrawal from *all* territories, while Israel insisted it had to hold onto *some* of the territories in order to live within secure boundaries.

In the immediate aftermath of the war, both Israel and the Arab states were divided with regard to how to proceed. The initial view of the Israeli government was that the conquered territory could be returned for peace, with the exception of those areas which Israel saw as strategically vital, as well as East Jerusalem. Opposition to territorial compromise was only expressed by Herut* and the National Religious Party*. Yet, as time proceeded without any indication of meaningful negotiations, 'the Israelis seemed increasingly reluctant to accept a formula which would require their complete withdrawal from territories occupied in war, even if their objectives of secure frontiers, non-belligerency and freedom of navigation were conceded' [76].

On the Arab side, the more hard-line states advocated a continuation of the conflict in order to liberate all of Palestine. Others, however, such as Nasser and King Hussein, preferred a diplomatic solution. The Arab summit in Khartoum in September 1967 decided the debate in favour of the hard-liners: No peace with, no recognition of, and no negotiation with, Israel [*Doc. 12*]. Despite the Khartoum resolution, the cause of the failure to resolve the conflict after the Six Day War was not Arab intransigence. Rather, it can be found in the continuing mutual distrust and in the enormous asymmetry of Israelis and Arabs, which precluded conditions conducive to negotiations from the beginning. Added to that was Israel's continued circumvention of the Palestinian refugees and their political representatives. Israel's strong position after the war did not encourage concessions, while the Arabs' weak position made it impossible to become an equal negotiating partner.

5 THE 1973 OCTOBER WAR

The unresolved Palestinian question, continuing border tension, the change in leadership in Egypt and Syria, intensified superpower interest in the region, and the failure of further diplomatic initiatives, paved the way for the fourth Arab–Israeli war. The conditions for conflict resolution after the 1967 war had simply not been right: the Arab states were unable to make peace from the position of utter defeat, Israel was unwilling to make concessions after its spectacular victory, the international community was unable to create an appropriate environment for negotiations, and the superpowers lacked the will and ability to impose peace [144]. It was in this context that the change of political leadership in Egypt provided a window of opportunity for a departure from entrenched positions.

THE WAR OF ATTRITION

In March 1969, Israel and Egypt had become involved in a prolonged low-intensity war known as the War of Attrition. In many ways it was a continuation of the 1967 war, and the Egyptian decision to launch this war can be seen as an attempt to break the deadlock. It was a conflict characterised by sporadic bombardment, commando raids, fire and counter-fire against strongholds along the Suez Canal. Egypt's principal aim was to keep the superpowers' interest alive – without that the reclaiming of the Suez Canal seemed impossible [104]. Nasser wanted to create sufficient instability to provoke superpower involvement and pressure the Soviet Union into supplying the Egyptian army with arms [11]. In that sense, Nasser's strategy was successful. Egypt received Soviet arms, technicians and combat personnel. In April 1970, Soviet pilots were detected flying Egyptian planes over the Suez Canal [65]. A further aim of Nasser was the destruction of the Israeli Bar Lev Line* fortification [99]. He sought to inflict such a heavy toll on Israel that it would be forced to withdraw. Between June 1967 and July 1970, more than 1,000 Israeli soldiers were killed [104].

Israel responded with bombardments of both military and civilian targets along the canal. By the middle of 1970 Egypt was sustaining considerable losses, and on 23 July Nasser accepted US Secretary of State Rogers' cease-fire proposal. On 8 August 1970 the War of Attrition came to an end. Nasser stated that he agreed to the cease-fire on the understanding that the United States would pressure Israel to accept Resolution 242 and withdraw from the occupied territories [65].

THE PALESTINIAN REVIVAL AND BLACK SEPTEMBER

On the Palestinian front, the 1967 war had made it clear that the Arab states were not able or willing to 'liberate' Palestine. Israel had gained control over more Palestinian land and a population of 665,000 Palestinians; an additional 350,000–400,000 Palestinians had become refugees. 'No one, least of all Israel, could dodge the problem of this new Palestinian actuality. The word "Arab" no longer served to describe everyone who was not Jewish. There were the "old" Arabs in Israel, the new West Bank–Gaza set, the militant fighters, and the various communities scattered in Lebanon, Jordan, Syria, and the Arabian Gulf' [116 *p. 38*]. Yet Resolution 242 failed seriously to address the situation of the Palestinian people and their political aspirations. As a result of the Arab defeat and international disregard of the Palestinian problem, the Palestinians became more independent politically, with Arafat emerging as the decisive voice among Palestinian leaders. It had become clear that the Palestinians could 'rely on no one but themselves' [136].

In winter 1967 Fatah started working underground in the West Bank, and the Arab–Israeli conflict, for the first time in 20 years, started to include an element of distinct Israeli–Palestinian confrontation, as exemplified by the battle of Karameh on 21 March 1968 which restored Palestinian morale. The ranks of the *fedayeen* of Fatah, as well as other organisations such as the Popular Front for the Liberation of Palestine (PFLP)*, swelled through an influx of volunteers.

Attempts at instigating an uprising in the West Bank were quickly crushed by the Israelis. The emerging Palestinian National Movement (PNM)* consequently had no choice but to operate from Jordan. In 1968 and 1969 Fatah established a network of proto-state institutions within Jordan including a political department, newspapers, grass-roots committees, and clinics which served politically to mobilise the population. Yasser Arafat was elected chairman of the executive committee as well as becoming the head of the PLO's political department. He set out to unify the resistance groups and to transform the PLO into a cohesive and comprehensive political front. The process of unification was completed in 1970 and the PLO was able to draw upon a fighting force of 5,000–10,000. Supported by states such as Saudi Arabia and Libya, the PLO stepped up its armed struggle against Israel.

The process of institutionalisation, structural and political development, and operational independence, increasingly set the PLO on a collision-course with the Lebanese and Jordanian governments. Palestinian attacks from Jordanian and Lebanese territory made Lebanon and Jordan the target of Israeli retaliatory strikes. There were an estimated 560 incidents initiated from the Lebanese side of the border in 1969–70 [136 p. 451].

Even more destabilising than Palestinian–Lebanese relations, were Palestinian–Jordanian relations. By 1970 the PLO had established a 'state within a state' in Jordan and had become a clear challenge to King Hussein's authority. Two unsuccessful assassination attempts on King Hussein by PFLP agents in early September and four spectacular airline hijackings were the final straw. On 17 September 1970, the Jordanian army moved against Palestinian positions. The *fedayeen* were unable to mount a credible defence. The fighting ended ten days later, on 27 September, when Nasser called a peace conference in Cairo. The Jordanian estimate of Palestinian fatalities was 1,500, while some Palestinian sources claim the number to be as high as 30,000. Inter-Arab relations had suffered a serious blow, which was further compounded when Nasser died of a heart attack the following day. Over the next year the PLO was ousted from Jordan, leaving Lebanon as the sole basis for free operations against Israel.

SYRO–EGYPTIAN PLANS FOR WAR

Sadat succeeded Nasser upon the latter's death on 28 September 1970. In an attempt to dissociate his leadership from Nasser's, Sadat initiated some crucial changes to Egypt's domestic and foreign policy, which had direct repercussions on the Arab–Israeli conflict. Nasser, according to Sadat, had reduced 'the revolution to a huge, dark and terrible pit, inspiring fear and hatred, but allowing no escape' and Nasser's economic legacy was 'in even poorer shape than the political' [65 p. 103]. As a result Sadat set out to de-Nasserise Egyptian politics and to improve the country's failing economy. Among the changes Sadat pursued was Egypt's relationship with the Soviet Union. Sadat had become increasingly disillusioned with Moscow's delayed arms supplies and consequently, on 18 July 1972, expelled 15,000 Russian military advisors. While this expulsion was a way to speed up Soviet arms shipments, to gain US favour, and to dissociate the Soviet Union from the upcoming war, Israel saw in this move an indication of Egyptian weakness. Indeed, 'at the beginning of 1973, Israel felt that American support and military aid, the decline in international pressure following the Munich Olympic massacre and Egypt's weakening links with Russia made an Arab attack unlikely' [99 *p. 216*].

At the same time Sadat started to pursue diplomatic initiatives to resolve the no war, no peace *status quo*. US Assistant Secretary of State, Joseph Sisco, recalls Israel's reaction to Sadat's 1971 proposals as follows: 'We met in the cabinet room around a huge conference table. Golda Meir, [Moshe] Dayan, [Abba] Eban, [Yitzhak] Rabin, [Yigal] Allon – the whole galaxy of Israeli high-level officials – were present. After two days of in-depth discussions, it was clear we weren't making much progress. I said, "But, Prime Minister, Sadat only wants a symbolic 500 riflemen across the Canal." But Golda Meir wouldn't budge' [23 *pp. 108–9*]. Sadat had offered to open the Suez Canal if Israel drew back from the canal, and to declare a cease-fire and sign a peace treaty with Israel based on UN Resolution 242 [104]. Israel, however, refused to withdraw to the pre-1967 armistice lines, believing that its new boundaries were vital for its national security. These diplomatic efforts not only failed to produce peace, they also contributed to the Israeli estimates that Egypt was not in a position to fight another war.

Yet despite the fact that Sadat knew that Egypt could not defeat Israel militarily, he opted to go to war in order to persuade Israel to make peace on terms acceptable to the Arabs. He had never intended the war to be more than a limited military operation, aimed at furthering his political and diplomatic objectives [136]. An attack on Israel would break the defeatist attitude of the population. It would boost his regional standing, and, if Egypt held its own, Sadat could use this more equal position as a basis for future negotiations with Israel. Talks with Israel were necessary as Sadat wanted to reclaim the Sinai and the Suez Canal for Egypt, especially as, three years after coming to power, he was still competing with Nasser's popular image. As Nasser had lost the Sinai in 1967, Sadat saw the recapture of the Sinai as the key to finally distinguish himself from Nasser. Further, an agreement with Israel would reduce the defence burden on the state. The Egyptian economy had virtually collapsed as a result of Nasser's state control, the cost of the Aswan Dam, the Yemen war, and the re-equipment of the Egyptian military after the 1967 war. And finally, an end of war between Egypt and Israel would create the stability required to attract foreign investment and would pave the way towards US economic aid.

On 30 November 1972, Sadat and Defence Minister General Ahmad Ismail Ali decided to go to war on the assumption that the superpowers would prevent a complete military victory by either side [99]. Sadat initiated private meetings with Hafez al-Asad in order to initiate a double front against Israel. On 31 January 1973, Syria's and Egypt's armed forces were placed under joint command. In an attempt to gain Arab backing for his plans, Sadat also consulted Saudi King Feisal, and Algerian President Boumedienne, as well as accepting a substantial financial contribution from Libya [99]. Detailed planning of the war began in March.

Syria's motivations in joining the war to some extent mirrored those of Egypt. Asad had manoeuvred himself into the presidency in 1970 and also saw a war as a way to consolidate his leadership. Asad's war aims, however, were mainly territorial. As he was the Defence Minister when the Golan Heights had been lost, he was determined to reclaim this territory from Israel. Unlike Sadat, Asad neither saw the war as a step towards a future agreement, nor did he want an end to the conflict with Israel.

A surprise attack was to catch Israel off-guard and leave it vulnerable, as the United States was paralysed by Watergate, was still suffering from its extrication from Vietnam, and Vice-President Spiro Agnew was facing tax charges.

THE 'SURPRISE' ATTACK

On 6 October 1973, at 2 p.m., Egypt and Syria attacked Israel. The war came as a surprise to Israel, to the extent that Israeli intelligence had failed to predict the confrontation despite evidence to the contrary. Israel had underestimated the frustration of the Arab governments over Israel's occupation of the Golan Heights, Sinai, West Bank and the Gaza Strip. It had also perceived the Arabs as weak, especially since Egypt had just expelled its Soviet military advisors. Sadat's repeated announcements that 1971 was the year of decision, without following through with action, further convinced Israel that Sadat's pronouncements were empty threats [104]. Indeed, Israeli military and political decision-makers had grown complacent, convinced of their own invincibility, and mobilisation of the Egyptian army had been interpreted as annual manoeuvres.

The Commander of the Armed Corps, General Avraham Adan, gives an insightful account into Israeli thinking at that time:

> My colleagues and I were certainly surprised. The underlying assessment of Israeli Intelligence was that the armed forces of the Arab nations were still unprepared for war; hence the probability of war seemed very low. For the past ten days, the Director of Military Intelligence had stuck to this evaluation, offering reasonable explanations about the build-up of forces. Moreover, the evening before, when he had briefed us about the evacuation of families of Soviet technicians from Egypt and Syria, he explained it as just the result of the widening gap between the Arabs and the Soviets. Now suddenly, without any signs of emotion or embarrassment, the DMI was predicting that war would erupt within hours [4 *p. 5*].

At 4 a.m. on 6 October, Defence Minister Dayan was informed that Egypt and Syria were going to attack and Israeli reserves were partially mobilised. A pre-emptive strike was ruled out, however, for fear that Israel would be seen as the aggressor and thereby alienate the United States. Israeli Prime Minister Golda Meir, in her autobiography, justified her position as follows: 'I know all the arguments in favour of a pre-emptive strike, but I am against it. We don't know now, any of us, what the future will hold, but there is always the possibility that we will need help, and if we strike first, we will get nothing from anyone' [89 *p. 359*]. Underlying her decision was the US concern about drawing the Soviet Union into the conflict, alienating Egypt, the possibility of an oil embargo, and involvement in yet another foreign war. Full mobilisation was also ruled out at that point. Israeli mobilisation earlier in the year had already placed a heavy burden on the economy and, being in the midst of a general election, the government could not risk further costs, should the attack not occur after all.

Egypt launched a massive airstrike and artillery assault on Israel, and Syria invaded the Golan Heights. Egyptian forces crossed the Suez Canal and pushed back Israeli troops. In the north, while Israel was still mobilising, Syria took Mount Hermon. In fact, the IDF was outnumbered 12 to 1 when the fighting began [104]. Mobilising Israel's forces was easy, as it was Yom Kippur*, the Jewish Day of Atonement, and most reservists were either at home or at the synagogue. In the first few days Israel came close to defeat and had been forced to withdraw from a number of positions. Although these Arab military accomplishments were unparalleled, the IDF managed to contain the threat [136]. A massive American airlift of military equip-

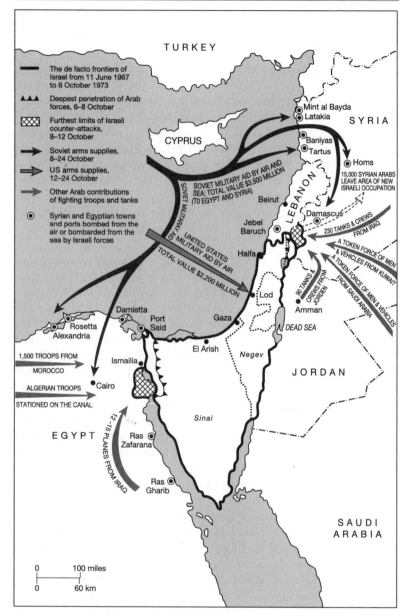

Legend:

— The de facto frontiers of Israel from 11 June 1967 to 6 October 1973

▲▲▲ Deepest penetration of Arab forces, 6–8 October

▨ Furthest limits of Israeli counter-attacks, 8–12 October

→ Soviet arms supplies, 8–24 October

⇒ US arms supplies, 12–24 October

→ Other Arab contributions of fighting troops and tanks

◉ Syrian and Egyptian towns and ports bombed from the air or bombarded from the sea by Israeli forces

TURKEY

CYPRUS

SYRIA

Mint al Bayda
Latakia
Baniyas
Tartus
Homs

15,000 SYRIAN ARABS LEAVE AREA OF NEW ISRAELI OCCUPATION

SOVIET MILITARY AID BY AIR AND SEA; TOTAL VALUE $3,500 MILLION (TO EGYPT AND SYRIA)

SOVIET MILITARY

Beirut

LEBANON

Damascus

230 TANKS & CREWS FROM IRAQ

Jebel Baruch

UNITED STATES MILITARY AID BY AIR TOTAL VALUE $2,200 MILLION

A TOKEN FORCE OF MEN & VEHICLES FROM KUWAIT

A TOKEN FORCE OF MEN & VEHICLES FROM SAUDI ARABIA

Haifa

Lod

90 TANKS & CREWS FROM JORDAN

Amman

Damietta
Rosetta
Alexandria

Port Said

Gaza

DEAD SEA

1,500 TROOPS FROM MOROCCO

Ismailia

El Arish

Negev

JORDAN

ALGERIAN TROOPS STATIONED ON THE CANAL

Cairo

EGYPT

12–15 PLANES FROM IRAQ

Ras Zafarana

Sinai

Ras Gharib

SAUDI ARABIA

0 ___ 100 miles
0 ___ 60 km

Map 3   The October war, 6–24 October 1973

ment combined with Israeli counter-offensives turned the tide [*Map* 3]. Washington had been reluctant to send arms during the first week of the conflict, fearing it might antagonise the Arabs, while also hoping that Israel might become more accommodating [54]. American reluctance was further influenced by the fact that US Secretary of State Henry Kissinger had received a message from Sadat stating that this war was only a limited operation aimed at forcing an Israeli withdrawal from the territories occupied in 1967, which would be followed by a peace settlement [47].

Syrian forces were repelled by 11 October and Israeli forces had crossed the Suez Canal by 18 October. Israeli forces were driving back the Arab armies [99]. It was at this point that the United States and the Soviet Union decided to impose a cease-fire. On 20 October, Kissinger flew to Moscow and drafted a cease-fire agreement with Communist Party Chairman Leonid Breznev. The cease-fire was accepted by all sides on 22 October. The last of the fighting ended on 24 October, but not before the Soviet Union had put its own troops on alert and threatened intervention in order to relieve the Egyptian Third Army, which had been trapped. This has led some analysts to assert that a superpower confrontation had been a distinct possibility. Others, however, have claimed that the Soviet Union had no intention of sending troops but wished only to put pressure on the United States to restrain Israel. The United States also only went on to red alert in order to disguise its compliance with this demand [144]. On 25 October, the Egyptian Third Army was resupplied; Arab dignity was saved and the United States was able to gain influence in Egypt, while Israel had still emerged victorious.

One final element of the war was the so-called oil weapon. Following the outbreak of the war, the Arab member-states of OPEC* stopped oil exports to the United States and the Netherlands, and reduced overall exports by 25 per cent. The embargo, which lasted until 1974, was designed to punish those states that were seen as overtly supportive of Israel, and served to boost Arab confidence further. Ultimately, however, it was the fact that the Arabs for the first time had not been militarily defeated, and the political gains from the war, which created conditions that were much more conducive to negotiations than at any time since 1948.

CONSEQUENCES OF THE WAR

Politically, the Arabs had won the war. Egyptian confidence had grown dramatically as a result of the war. From an Egyptian perspective, Israel had only been saved by the United States. The belief in Israel's invincibility had been destroyed. Moreover, Sadat had acquired the international reputation of an accomplished political strategist. 'Sadat emerged from the war a world statesman, something Nasser aspired to but never achieved' [99 *p. 221*]. He was hailed as the 'hero of the crossing'.

Despite the Israeli victory, confidence had been seriously shaken, resulting in public anger directed at Prime Minister Golda Meir and Defence Minister Moshe Dayan, and leading to a full investigation of the intelligence failure under the Agranat Commission. The Commission's report was highly critical of military intelligence, discipline and training, but failed to address the responsibility of political leaders for Israel's losses [136].

At the same time, human losses and a general feeling of uncertainty strengthened the search for a settlement. An estimated 3,000 Israeli and 8,500 Egyptian and Syrian soldiers were killed, and 8,000 Israelis and almost 20,000 Syrians wounded [104 *p. 74*]. It was the first Arab–Israeli war in which Israel suffered a high casualty rate, had men missing in action and prisoners were taken by the enemy [4]. These traumatic effects led to the emergence of an Israeli peace movement.

Ironically, the insecurity created by the war also gave rise to Israel's religious right. Thus it was not the victorious Six Day War which led to a government-backed settlement policy for ideological rather than security reasons, but the despair of the Yom Kippur War which resulted in reviving the notion of a greater 'Eretz Yisrael' (Land of Israel)* [35]. Consequently, groups such as Gush Emunim* started to gain prominence.

Above all, Sadat had made it clear that Egypt was ready for a settlement with Israel, and Syria was willing now to accept UN resolution 242. US Secretary of State and President Richard Nixon's national security advisor Henry Kissinger was convinced that both Egypt and Syria were ready for compromise. Israel too, being in economic and political turmoil, was believed to be more flexible.

The United Nations was at the forefront of attempts to restart negotiations with UN Resolution 338 [*Doc. 13*], which was passed when the cease-fire was ordered on 22 October 1973. The resolution called for the immediate termination of all military activity, and implementation of UN resolution 242. In December, Soviet and American foreign ministers convened a Middle East peace conference in Geneva. However, this initiative accomplished little. In fact, it has been argued that Kissinger only backed the Geneva conference in order to give the Soviets the impression of co-operation, before he pursued direct talks with the Sadat and Meir governments [131]. Nevertheless, the groundwork for Kissinger's famous shuttle diplomacy had been laid.

6   THE EGYPTIAN–ISRAELI PEACE PROCESS

The shift from conflict to negotiation, or from war to peace, has proved a particularly difficult one in the context of protracted conflict. Indeed, continuing a war can be the most comfortable option as it represents an almost predictable certainty in the face of the uncertainties of peace and change. In most cases the decision to engage in a peace process has been motivated by a stalemate which makes it clear that neither side can completely defeat the other, the presence of spokespersons for both sides, and the availability of a formula for the way out [145]. The 1973 October war presented the possibility for all of these. Renewed military confrontation made it clear, on the one hand, that Egypt could not defeat Israel despite the element of surprise and acquisition of Soviet arms, and, on the other hand, that Israel, despite being victorious in all Arab–Israeli wars, was not protected from Arab attacks. Further, US Secretary of State Henry Kissinger's determination to find a settlement provided both sides with a formula which made it easy to move beyond a disengagement agreement. And finally, the determination of President Anwar Sadat and the willingness of Israeli Prime Minister Menachem Begin to take the risks of peace made successful Israeli–Egyptian negotiations possible.

DISENGAGEMENT

Attempts at restarting negotiations began with the cease-fire on 22 October and UN resolution 338 [*Doc. 13*]. On 11 November 1973 the first agreement between Israel and Egypt was reached at kilometre 101 on the Cairo–Suez road. It provided for relief for the Egyptian Third Army trapped behind Israeli lines, the replacement of Israeli by UN checkpoints, and the exchange of prisoners [47]. Equally, or even more important, it marked a change in Egyptian–Israeli relations exemplified by Egyptian Chief of Staff General Abdel Ghani Gamasy, who said to Israeli Deputy Chief of Staff Israel Tal: 'Look, this is the first time that a war has ended between us in equality. We can say we won and can say it's a tie. From this position we can negotiate. This time we want to end the conflict' [23 *p. 126*]. In December 1973, the United Nations, the United States and the Soviet Union convened a Middle East Peace Conference in Geneva. According to Kissinger, 'The Geneva Conference was a way to get all parties into harness for one symbolic act, thereby to enable each to pursue a separate course' [73 *p. 747*]. However, the conference, failed to reconvene after the opening speeches. It accomplished little, apart from providing the professional diplomats with a 'testing ground for all the arcane knowledge acquired in a lifetime of study about procedures, about abstruse points of protocol, about "auspices" and "chairmanship"' [73 *p. 755*].

Behind the scenes Kissinger continued to work towards disengagement along the Suez Canal in order to stabilise the situation. In principle, Kissinger was still operating within the framework of the United Nations. In practice, however, he had by-passed both the United Nations and the Russians, when he embarked upon his shuttle diplomacy following the collapse of the Geneva conference [131]. He was convinced that he could achieve at least partial agreements, based upon a step-by-step approach and a land-for-peace basis. So 'the US diplomat tirelessly shuttled back and forth between Jerusalem, Cairo, and Damascus' [136 p. 481]. He told Israel that the conclusion of an agreement would reduce pressure for further concessions, while, at the same time, he told the Arabs that partial Israeli withdrawal would ultimately lead to complete Israeli withdrawal. Kissinger's persistence and negotiating skills were successful. On 18 January 1974, the Disengagement of Forces Agreement', or Sinai I, between Egypt and Israel was signed. It provided for the withdrawal of Israeli forces from the west bank of the canal. A second Israeli accord with Egypt, known as the Sinai II Accord, was signed on 1 September 1975, enabling Cairo to regain more control over the Sinai peninsula, including the oilfields. US President Gerald Ford, who had succeeded Nixon upon his resignation in August 1974, had been disappointed with the Israeli unwillingness to make concessions in Sinai II; the Israeli approach 'frustrated the Egyptians and made me mad as hell' while 'Kissinger's exasperation with [Yitzhak] Rabin knew no bounds' [12 *p. 346;* 46 *p. 249*].

The disengagement agreement with Syria had been even more difficult than the Israeli–Egyptian one. Damascus had adopted a hard-line view, and border clashes continued for months after the cease-fire [104]. These tensions between Syria and Israel made it difficult to pursue settlement beyond disengagement. Hafez al-Asad had little interest in negotiations with Israel unless the Arabs formed a united front, and consequently viewed Sadat's willingness to pursue an agreement with deep suspicion. On the one hand, he feared that Egypt's willingness to compromise would undermine his own efforts to regain all the territory of the Golan Heights. On the other, he saw this as an opportunity to make his bid for Arab leadership. The realignment of regional powers consequently saw a decline in Syrian–Egyptian relations, while Syria realigned itself with Iraq, Algeria, Libya, South Yemen and the PLO [104].

Israeli–Syrian negotiations took place against the backdrop of Israeli domestic problems. Prime Minister Golda Meir resigned in April 1974 and was succeeded by former Chief of Staff General Yitzhak Rabin. For Israel an agreement with Syria proved more difficult as the Golan Heights had posed a close threat. Indeed, neither side had much territory to spare. The Israeli agreement to withdraw from just beyond Quneitra on the Golan Heights was finally secured on 31 May 1974. 'What really persuaded the Israelis was Kissinger's clever mixture of threats and secret assurances' [47 *p. 110*]. It had also, however, become clear that Syrian–Israeli negotiations would go no further. Kissinger's assessment of this situation was that 'to Sadat, disengagement was the first step in what he suspected, given Syrian ambivalence, would have to be a separate Egyptian peace; Asad probably rationalised that it was the last phase prior to a renewed confrontation with Israel' [73 *p. 748*].

THE 1977 LIKUD VICTORY

In June 1977 Menachem Begin became prime minister of the first Likud government since the establishment of the state of Israel. The shift within the Israeli electorate was the result of voter dissatisfaction with the Labour Alignment which had been racked by rivalries and scandals [136]. It also marked the political coming-of-age of the second generation of Jews of Afro–Asian origin. Having originated from Muslim countries, they were more likely to regard the Arabs as untrustworthy and to oppose territorial concessions. Indeed, it has been claimed that their ideological contribution has been 'populist chauvinism and crude anti-Arab sentiment' [133 *p. 15*]. Their experience with Labour leaders during the 1950s and 1960s was one of being treated as culturally inferior and being housed in transition camps for prolonged periods. This further contributed to the election victory of the Likud.

The election signalled a change in Israeli domestic policy. The general expectation was that this would be a change towards intransigence and militancy. Indeed, with 'Begin in power, it was feared, the chances of a political settlement of the Arab–Israeli conflict had been ruined, and the probability of a new war had grown' [16 *p. 19*]. This perception was based on the fact that Likud policy marked a significant departure from previous Labour governments with its commitment to Judea and Samaria (the West Bank). As heir of the Jewish underground organisation Irgun during the time of the British mandate, and indebted to Vladimir Jabotinsky's revisionist philosophy, the party emphasised national security and contained an anti-Arab element. Its ideological platform advocated an aggressive settlement policy of the West Bank on the grounds that this territory was an integral part of Israel. Arabs in this territory, and even those within the pre-1967 boundaries, the so-called Green Line*, were regarded as alien to the country. Likud's approach was one of territorial maximalism* combined with a strong reliance on military power based on the beliefs of the indivisibility of the Land of Israel, hostility towards Arabs, never-ending war against the PLO, and 'a constant siege mentality along with enthusiastic utterances about religious redemption' [133 *p. 16*]. Accordingly, Begin made it clear that Israel was going to retain the Golan Heights, hold on to the West Bank, and to exclude the Palestinians from negotiations. It is therefore not surprising that observers at the time of Begin's election regarded the defeat of Labour as a major setback for peace in the region. Yet, at the same time, Begin, while still prime minister elect, approached US Ambassador to Israel Samuel Lewis and told him that his first aim as prime minister would be negotiations with Egypt [16]. Thus Sadat's belief that the time was 'ripe' for peace was not unfounded.

On 9 November 1977, following several months of painfully slow, secret Israeli–Egyptian negotiations through the mediation of King Hassan II of Morocco, Sadat announced to the Egyptian National Assembly that he was willing to go to Israel and address the Israeli Knesset [*Doc. 14*] in order to get the ball rolling again. It has been claimed that US President Jimmy Carter's insistence on including the Russians through the Geneva conference, pushed Sadat into going to Jerusalem in order to pre-empt Soviet involvement. Another motivation cited for Sadat's decision to make this unprecedented move, is Israeli intelligence information about a Libyan plot against his life, which was passed to him through King Hassan [99]. Now that the ball was in Israel's court Begin, in a sense, had no choice but to accept. Israeli Defence Minister Ezer Weizman pointed out the irony in his memoirs. 'The first offer [for peace] had come and met with a response under Begin's leadership. ... Begin's reputation was that of a superhawk, a right-wing extremist, and Herut was perceived as a party of war. As it turned out, it was only because Begin was such a blatantly self-declared hawk that he could get away with taking chances' [140 *pp. 23–4*].

On 19 November, Sadat arrived in Jerusalem to discuss peace. It was the first official, direct and public contact between an Arab state and Israel, breaking down some of the psychological barriers which had existed since 1948. Yet the American government remained dubious that Sadat and Begin could reach an agreement without third party mediation, especially since it had become obvious that Sadat liked neither Begin nor Foreign Minister Moshe Dayan, preferring Defence Minister Ezer Weizman instead.

Of particular interest within the emerging negotiations are the different – and to some degree conflicting – visions of the outcome of the talks. When US President Jimmy Carter took office in 1976, it was clear that he intended to play a more active role in the Middle East and to introduce some of his own ideas into US policy. Carter's conception of a settlement included the resolution of the Palestinian problem, substantive Israeli territorial concessions, Arab recognition of Israel, as well as Soviet involvement as a mediator. Carter's ideas differed significantly from those previously held by Kissinger, who had neither considered the PLO a factor in the peace process nor believed that the Soviet Union had a role to play. Carter tried to provide the peace process with new direction, a direction which was to some extent at odds with Egypt and Israel.

A change in Israeli views had also taken place over the period of negotiations. Yitzhak Rabin, who was the Israeli prime minister during the first stages of the US mediation beginning in January 1977, declared that he could compromise on the territory of the Sinai, but there would be no concessions on the Golan Heights. The issues of Palestinian inclusion into talks, and the West Bank, were kept vague. Once Begin took office in June 1977, the status of the West Bank was clarified. Begin had run on an electoral platform which considered the West Bank to be an integral part of the Land of Israel. He also opposed the inclusion of the PLO in negotiations, equating Yasser Arafat with Hitler.

Sadat outlined his idea of a settlement in his speech to the Knesset. He wanted neither a separate or partial peace, nor a third disengagement agreement. Instead, he wanted a 'durable peace based on justice'. Such a settlement would require the Israeli withdrawal from the territories captured in the 1967 June War and the Palestinian right to self-determination. Despite the historic connotations, Begin was determined not to be 'swayed by the emotion of the moment into making concessions he would later regret' [47 *p. 122*].

Sadat's visit to Jerusalem in November 1977, which has been described as one of the most remarkable events of the post-war era [11], sparked another round of intense Israeli–Egyptian–US diplomacy, including a visit by Begin to Ismailia on Christmas Day 1977. The Ismailia conference, however, ended in failure. 'It had also highlighted the glaring differences between the leaders on either side. Sadat had hoped the conference would bring about an understanding in principle. He'd offered Israel full peace – in return for withdrawal from the Sinai and an understanding over the Palestinians. ... As for Begin, he had ignored principles, plunging into details instead, most of which scarcely interested the Egyptian president' [140 *p. 136*].

In early 1978, it became clear that Israeli–Egyptian talks had become deadlocked over the issue of the West Bank and Palestinian rights to self-rule, proving American fears correct. In an attempt to break this deadlock, Carter decided to convene a summit at Camp David in September 1978 in order 'to save the peace'.

THE CAMP DAVID ACCORDS

The Carter Administration, with all its faults in other areas of policy-making, was able to provide the environment that made Egyptian–Israeli peace negotiations possible. It displayed an almost unprecedented degree of consensus, between the president, Secretary of State Cyrus Vance and National Security Advisor Zbigniew Brzezinski.

The potential for stalemate had become clear soon after Sadat's visit to Jerusalem. Israel, in an attempt to retain the West Bank, blocked any proposed clauses which could be interpreted in favour of an independent Palestinian entity, while Egypt demanded Israeli recognition of the Palestinian right to self-rule [131]. Begin was only willing to concede administrative autonomy: in essence, control over health, welfare and education [104]. In a move to break the impasse, Carter called a summit at Camp David, which Israel and Egypt were unable to refuse as the invitation had been from the US president personally [139]. The diplomatic exchanges, which lasted from 5 to 17 September, were intense and the atmosphere was not always the most cordial. Indeed, two days before the end of the negotiations Sadat threatened to withdraw.

Nevertheless, two agreements were concluded and signed in 'an emotional ceremony in the East Room of the White House late on 17 September 1978' [11 *p. 357*]. The first comprised the principles for an

Egyptian–Israeli peace treaty and normalisation of relations [*Doc. 15*]. Israel would give up the Sinai, including settlements and airfields. The second provided a 'Framework for Peace in the Middle East', based on Resolutions 242 and 338, the resolution of the Palestinian problem, good neighbourly relations, and Palestinian autonomy in the West Bank (excluding Jerusalem) and Gaza Strip [*Doc. 15*].

According to Carter's and Sadat's interpretation of Palestinian autonomy, a Palestinian self-governing authority, freely elected by the inhabitants of the West Bank and Gaza Strip, should replace the Israeli military administration. During a five-year transition period the final status of the territories should be negotiated [99]. Carter genuinely believed that he had obtained a major concession on the West Bank, but Begin interpreted Palestinian autonomy as no more than 'personal autonomy' [47].

Both Begin and Sadat had difficulties convincing the public that the concessions made were justified. Sadat had cut Egypt off from the rest of the Arab world, while Begin was faced with the emergence of a new radical right consisting of the newly established Tehiya* party, Gush Emunim, the Land of Israel Movement*, and Kach* who were determined to fight against Camp David. Despite these obstacles, Sadat and Begin were able to achieve legitimacy in the eyes of most Egyptians and most Israelis respectively.

On 26 March 1979 the Egyptian–Israeli peace treaty was signed. Israel returned the Sinai to Egypt in return for peace, full diplomatic relations, and shipping through the Suez Canal and Gulf of Aqaba. In the months following the treaty, it became clear that Begin had no intention of relinquishing Israeli control over the West Bank and Gaza Strip. The continuation and indeed increase of Israeli settlement activity confirmed this. It is thus not surprising that the negotiations on the autonomy scheme only continued for a short period and were suspended by the end of 1979. The Carter administration was unable to put pressure on Israel, because it became caught up in the emerging Iranian Revolution, the US hostage crisis in November 1979, the Soviet invasion of Afghanistan in December, and upcoming presidential elections.

IMPLICATIONS OF PEACE

Arab leaders were caught between a rock and a hard place. They had to decide whether it was better to be left out of negotiations or to participate in them. In the end only Egypt proceeded, and the general Arab reaction to the Israeli–Egyptian peace turned into one of open hostility. The exclusion of the Palestinians, in particular, provided a rallying point. While Arab leaders now sought to fill the regional leadership vacuum by declaring sympathy with the Palestinians, the PLO became more determined in its quest for Palestinian self-determination. Prominent Palestinian scholar Edward Said's assessment of the autonomy provisions of the Camp David Agreement reflects popular Palestinian feelings at that time: 'You cannot expect millions of Arab Palestinians to go away, or to be content with occupation, or to acquiesce to an Israeli, or an Egyptian, or an American, idea for their destiny, their "autonomy", or their physical location.' For the West Bank Palestinians, the Egyptian–Israeli agreement seemed to confirm continued Israeli rule over them, declared openly by Begin himself, whatever the expectations of Carter and Sadat [131].

The implications of peace for Egypt were both positive and negative. The Arab League imposed a political and economic boycott on Egypt, and moved its headquarters from Cairo to Tunis. Egypt's membership in the Arab League was suspended and Egypt became ostracised. The suspension of negotiations on the West Bank led to the charge that Sadat 'had abandoned the Palestinian cause in order to recover the Sinai' [136 *p. 514*]. The lack of rapid economic growth which had been promised to the Egyptian population left him open to further criticism. In the end, Sadat paid the ultimate price for peace with Israel. He was assassinated on 6 October 1981 by members of the Islamist organisation Takfir wa al-Hijra* as he reviewed a parade to commemorate the crossing of the Suez Canal.

Yet despite Sadat's assassination and the pervading disaffection of Egyptians and hostility of most other Arabs, Sadat's successor Hosni Mubarak upheld the peace agreement with Israel. Egypt thus became the first Arab state to make peace with Israel. The Egyptian boycott against Israel was lifted, embassies were opened, regular airline flights began in March 1980, and Egypt started selling oil to Israel. Both Egypt and Israel benefited from the peace in terms of US aid and support. And as early as 1974, after the first disengagement agreement had been concluded, US President Richard Nixon had offered both Egypt and Israel help with civil nuclear power [11]. Finally, in the long-run, Sadat's peace initiative also made it possible for Egypt to emerge as the key Arab mediator in the 1991 Middle East Peace Process.

Peace had less equivocal benefits for Israel. The Knesset's massive support for the treaty with Egypt vindicated Begin's decision to return the Sinai. It provided Israel with security and stability along its southern border and thereby freed-up the country's limited resources. The peace agreement had removed the Arab country with the largest military force from the Arab–Israeli conflict, and precluded a two-front option against Israel.

Normalisation became the most important Israeli aim after the treaty had been signed. The main stumbling block on this front remained Israeli–Egyptian friction over Palestinian autonomy. Israel's continued settlement policy, the 1981 annexation of the Golan Heights and the stalemate in the autonomy talks, as well as Israel's 1982 invasion of Lebanon, soon turned the two states' relations into a cold peace.

7   THE 1982 LEBANON WAR

After 1970, peace and stability along Israel's border with Lebanon became paramount for Israel's security. The expulsion of the PLO from Jordan to Lebanon after Black September increasingly became a threat to Israeli interests. The Lebanese civil war which erupted in 1975 further heightened Israeli concerns. The war raised the distinct possibility that Lebanon could fall to the PLO, end up under Syrian control, or that civil unrest could contaminate the region as a whole. It is therefore not surprising that when Lebanon's Maronite Christians appealed for aid from Israel, Israel seized upon the opportunity to influence events in Lebanon. The initially cautious approach of the Rabin government was soon replaced by the committed stance of the Begin government. Peace with Egypt, moreover, freed Israel to focus on the north. As a result, what had started as a spate of retaliatory raids against Palestinian *fedayeen*, developed into a grand strategy through which Israel sought to change the geo-strategic make-up of the Middle East. Israel's 1982 invasion of Lebanon was the means to this end.

THE LEBANESE CIVIL WAR

In 1975, yet another Lebanese political crisis was unleashed during a strike of Sidon fishermen. Soldiers trying to remove a roadblock were ambushed. Tensions spread north when Maronite Kataib* party leader Pierre Gemayel was fired at by Palestinians on 13 April. In retaliation, the Kataib attacked a Palestinian bus passing through the Beirut suburb Ain al-Rummana. This incident sparked off further clashes between Palestinians and Christians; the Lebanese civil war had begun.

At the heart of the conflict was the political and socio-economic power-imbalance between Christian and Muslim communities. One of the main problems which had led to the unrest, was that of minority-majority integration. Instead of the political leaders balancing the interests of the different communities in the true sense of Lebanon's consociational democracy, and thereby creating a basis for a wider Lebanese identity, they pursued their own limited agendas, resulting in communal distrust. The other key issue was the still unresolved question of Lebanon's identity as an Arab, Mediterranean or Christian state.

Constructed upon a system in which government offices were allocated on communal grounds based on a census conducted in 1932, Maronite Christians traditionally held the presidency, Sunni Muslims the premiership, and Shi'a Muslims the position of the Speaker of the House. Since 1932 the demographic realities, however, had not only shifted in favour of Lebanon's economically disadvantaged Shi'as, but the inter-communal balance had also been tipped by the influx of an estimated 270,000 Palestinian refugees [104]. Lebanon's Christians feared political changes which would denigrate them to the second-class position Christians occupied in other Muslim-majority states. They saw the *status quo* as the only guarantee for their religious and cultural freedom. At the same time Lebanon's Muslims – Sunni, Shi'a and Druze – were pushing for political reform.

The state started to disintegrate when the different ethno-religious communities lost trust in the formal institutions, which they no longer believed to be powerful or impartial enough to protect their respective interests [120]. Sectarian allegiances emerged as the primary affiliation even before the 1975–76 war when the political system was suffering from the strains of rapid development. Increasing pressure for fairer representation and equitable distribution of wealth and status, came to be supported by sectarian militias.

In an effort to stop the sectarian conflict from both destroying Lebanon and spilling over into neighbouring Syria, Asad sent Syrian troops into Lebanon in 1976. For Asad, Lebanon's troubles provided the perfect opportunity not only to prevent the possibility of future Lebanese military rule but also to assert control over Palestinian forces and to deter Israel from filling the power vacuum. In addition, Asad's shrewd move brought Syria one step closer to fulfilling its territorial claims as well as once again demonstrating that he himself was the most effective Arab leader in the region. Thus in the context of regional dynamics, Lebanon became a key factor in the Syrian–Israeli deterrence dialogue. It also became a surrogate battlefield for the Israeli–Palestinian conflict after the PLO's move to Beirut.

LIMITED ISRAELI INTERVENTION

Border clashes between Palestinian *fedayeen* and Israelis had steadily increased from the early 1970s onwards. The resulting instability led the Christian population in South Lebanon to appeal for Israeli aid. This was provided in the form of weapons, food and medication known as the 'Good Fence' policy, which was a strategic response to the Lebanese government's lack of control over the South. In March 1976, Lebanese army officer Saad Haddad started to establish the so-called South Lebanese Army (SLA)*, approved of and later supported by Israel [42].

The first large-scale Israeli military intervention was Operation Litani. It was launched in response to a Palestinian attack on an Israeli bus on the Haifa–Tel Aviv road on 11 March 1978. This incident in the heart of the country, in which 37 Israelis died and another 78 were wounded, resulted in a new direction in Israel's Lebanon policy. The main objectives of Operation Litani were the punishment of the PLO and the destruction of the PLO infrastructure south of the Litani river. A further objective added during the operation was the creation of a security zone in co-operation with Haddad's forces.

Parallel to the developments in South Lebanon, Israel's relationship with Beirut politician Bashir Gemayel, son of Kataib leader Pierre Gemayel, began to solidify in 1977. Bashir Gemayel's aims were to build a free Lebanon – free of Syrian troops, free of Palestinian *fedayeen*, and free of stifling feudal traditions. His first two aims coincided with Israel's security interests, providing a basis for increased collaboration. In practical terms this meant weapons, training and military advisors for Bashir's forces. This stronger Israeli commitment was also reflected in Prime Minister Begin's statements. He publicly announced, 'we shall not, under any circumstances, abandon the Christians into the hands of their tormentors' [88 *p. 287*].

Bashir Gemayel proceeded with unifying all Christian militias into the Lebanese Front. For the first time optimism and a determined strategy were visible in the Christian camp. 'If a unified Lebanon could be maintained, which would preserve the ethos and power structure of the traditional Lebanese entity, then the Front should strive for it. If that were not the case, the "smaller Lebanon" strategy should be resorted to' [109 *p. 114*].

Israeli–Maronite relations from 1977 to 1980 developed from covert connections into an overt alliance aided by the unification of the Maronite forces and the Likud government's interventionist approach, as well as the consolidation of the PLO in Lebanon. Maronite and Israeli interests started to converge around common aims and enemies. Syrian and Palestinian forces needed to be ejected from Lebanon and a stable Maronite-dominated state needed to be re-established.

OPERATION PEACE FOR GALILEE

Regional and domestic Israeli changes in 1981 and 1982 paved the way for Israel's invasion of Lebanon. In 1981 Israel's government was reshuffled. Foreign Minister Moshe Dayan was succeeded by Itzhak Shamir, and Defence Minister Ezer Weizman by Ariel Sharon. Both Dayan and Weizman had served as a restraining force, while Shamir and Sharon had the opposite effect, thus increasing the preference for a military option [124]. The second factor increasing the likelihood for an Israeli invasion was a two-week war of attrition between Palestinian guerrillas firing rockets at Israel's north, and the IDF and SLA shelling Palestinian positions. An estimated 5,000 Israeli families fled the area, revealing Israel's vulnerability. This two-week war in June 1981 was followed by a US-mediated cease-fire, which in Israeli eyes had deprived the IDF of the option to take punitive action [122]. Moreover, the ability of the PLO to maintain this cease-fire increased Arafat's international standing and thus increased the Palestinian nationalist threat. It was at this point that the decision to launch another ground operation was taken.

The regional and international environments were also conducive to Israeli military action. The last stage of Egyptian–Israeli peace negotiations had finally been concluded, so Israel could focus on its northern border. War with Syria was also considered to be on the cards in the near future, so why not engage the Syrians on Israel's terms? And finally, the US administration, in particular Secretary of State Alexander Haig, had not openly opposed Israeli invasion plans when Israel's ambassador to Washington tested US reaction. Indeed, in a meeting between Haig and Sharon on 25 May 1982 when Sharon briefed the Secretary of State on the possibility of an Israeli ground operation, Haig only told Sharon that nothing should be done without clear provocation [23 *p. 166*]. Sharon did not have to wait long. On 3 June, Israeli Ambassador Shlomo Argov was shot outside the Dorchester Hotel in London. The assassination attempt was traced to Abu Nidal's Palestinian faction but as Begin considered the PLO to be ultimately responsible for all Palestinian actions and Sharon could not let this 'clear provocation' pass, the ball for Israel's invasion of Lebanon was set rolling.

Plans for the invasion had already been co-ordinated between Sharon and Bashir Gemayel in January 1982. They had discussed linking up Bashir's quest for the presidency with a large-scale Israeli operation. Sharon proposed to eliminate the PLO from Lebanon with the aid of the Lebanese Forces, after which a political solution would be possible [124]. So using the 3 June assassination attempt on Israel's ambassador in London as a pretext, Israel invaded Lebanon on 6 June 1982. Defence Minister Ariel Sharon declared the goal of the war to be the elimination of the PLO in South Lebanon [104], but by the time the first cease-fire was called Israeli troops were already on the outskirts of Beirut [*Map 4*]. It soon became clear that Operation Peace for Galilee had much broader aims: first, eliminating all Palestinian presence and influence from Lebanon; secondly, creating a new political order in Lebanon by establishing a Maronite government under Bashir Gemayel; thirdly, the expulsion of Syrian troops; fourthly, the destruction of Palestinian nationalism in the West Bank and Gaza Strip; and finally, the freeing of Israel from past traumas such as the 1973 war [102; 37; 109]. Ironically, peace for Galilee was not the main objective; rather, it was a basic change in Israel's regional position.

The IDF advanced towards Beirut, engaging both Palestinian and Syrian forces on its way to linking up with the Lebanese Forces. The plan envisaged that the Lebanese Forces would deal with Muslim West Beirut and thereby make it unnecessary for Israeli forces to enter the city. But when Israeli and Maronite troops joined up at Ba'abda, Bashir made it clear to Sharon that he had no intention of fulfilling his side of the bargain [19]. He was willing to aid the IDF, but not to engage in combat, in order not to jeopardise his election. After all, he wanted to become president of *all* of Lebanon. As a result, Israel had to deal with the PLO in West Beirut itself.

On 1 July, Israeli troops laid siege to the city, despite the fact that a cease-fire had technically been in place for six days. The siege was aimed at striking a mortal blow to an estimated 12,000–14,000 PLO fighters [49]. It started with a concerted campaign of psychological warfare consisting of leaflets and mock bomb-runs to convince the PLO that an attack was imminent. US mediator Philip Habib, who had been sent in to defuse the crisis, had achieved little. The PLO was determined to stay in Beirut, while the IDF was equally determined to evict it. On 3 July, the IDF sealed off West Beirut and opened tank and artillery fire on Palestinian positions. As the siege continued, Israel cut off water, food supplies and fuel. Gunboats began to shell West Beirut and rocket exchanges broke out between the PLO and the IDF. As the fighting increased, Habib continued to press for an agreement behind the scenes. On 6 August, a commitment to PLO withdrawal was finally secured. But it was not until 22 August that the

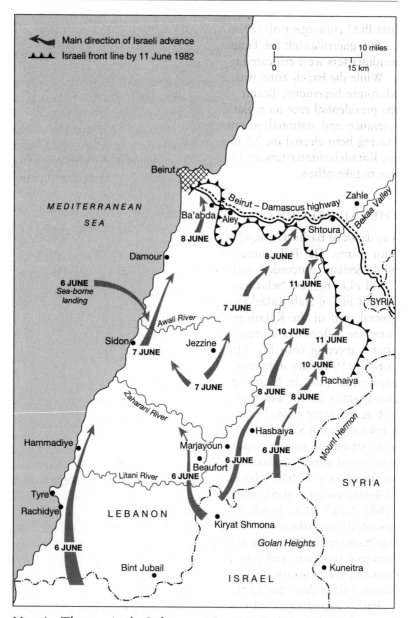

Map 4   The war in the Lebanon, 6 June–21 August 1982

first PLO contingent of 379 men departed from Beirut [49]. In total, 11,000 guerrillas left for Tunisia, Algeria, Yemen and Syria, and PLO headquarters were relocated to Tunis.

While the Israeli army was 'liberating' Lebanon in order to restore Maronite hegemony, Bashir Gemayel denounced Israel and entered the presidential race on a platform of cross-community co-operation, tolerance and national reconciliation. His success was short-lived. Having been elected on 23 August, he was killed in the bombing of the Kataib headquarters on 14 September 1982, a week before he was due to take office.

THE FAILURES OF OPERATION PEACE FOR GALILEE

The death of Bashir Gemayel was also the death knell for Israel's Lebanon plans. The IDF immediately moved towards the Green Line, while Sharon proceeded with his plans to get rid of an estimated 2,000 PLO fighters 'who had gone civilian' [71]. On 15 September, Israeli Chief of Staff Rafael Eitan and General Amir Drori met with the general staff of the Kataib militia and agreed that the latter would enter the Palestinian camps [85]. The next day, on 16 September, after a meeting with Elie Hobeika and Fadi Frem of the Lebanese Forces, 150 Kataib militiamen entered Sabra and Shatilla under IDF supervision [20]. In Eitan's words they were 'eager to take revenge [for Bashir's death] and there may be rivers of blood' [102 p. 162]. Yet at the same time, he publicly maintained that the 'IDF had no knowledge until Saturday morning of what was going on' [85 p. 168]. This statement was contradicted by Israeli and foreign journalists who heard about the massacre on the Friday morning. Estimates of the dead vary widely. The Israeli Kahan Commission claimed that 700–800 civilians died, while others place the number as high as 1,500–2,000 [68]. Israeli journalists Zeev Schiff and Ehud Ya'ari described the massacres as the 'wholesale slaughter of families', including 'hanging live grenades around their victims' necks', infants being trampled to death, and rape [122 p. 264]. Far from 'guerrillas gone civilian', the majority of the victims were women and children, and almost half of them Shi'a Lebanese [58 p. 176].

Bashir Gemayel's death was a crucial turning point. No other Maronite leader combined the ability to govern Lebanon with a political orientation acceptable to Israel. His brother Amin who succeeded him not only had a different political vision, he also did not want an alliance with Israel, courted good relations with the Arab world, and preferred to rely on US mediation.

The failure of Operation Peace for Galilee, however, was ultimately the result of Israeli misconceptions. Israel had based its plans on the illusion of Bashir Gemayel's power in the Maronite community and the power of the Maronites in Lebanon. Further, Israeli decision-makers failed to understand Maronite goals. Maronite non-co-operation, once Israel had entered Lebanon, compounded by Bashir Gemayel's death and the lack of contingency plans, placed Israel in an unenviable position.

THE 1983 MAY 17TH AGREEMENT

Through US mediation, official negotiations between Israel and Lebanon began on 28 December 1982. To Israel's chagrin, Amin Gemayel not only insisted upon including Shi'a and Sunni representatives in the negotiations, he also refused to agree a single word without first having the approval of the Sunni prime minister [71 *p. 159*].

The domestic outcry over the Sabra and Shatilla massacres made it imperative for Israel to produce a treaty in order to justify the war. But differences in Lebanese and Israeli positions soon became apparent. Israel wanted security for its northern border, full diplomatic relations and normalisation. Lebanon, in contrast, wanted to minimise contact with Israel and, above all, wanted Israeli withdrawal. The agreement [*Doc. 18*] that was signed on 17 May 1983 fell short of both Israel's security and Lebanon's political requirements. The treaty terminated the war without installing peace, but guaranteed respect for territorial sovereignty and political independence. The secret annex dealt more specifically with the security arrangements. The southern boundary of the security zone was defined as the international border between Israel and Lebanon, the northern boundary as the Awali river. For Israel it was no more than a glorified armistice agreement which it felt compelled to ratify in light of the economic and political burden of the occupation and mounting casualties.

Lebanon was in an equally difficult position. Amin Gemayel had sought US mediation in order to achieve not only Israeli but ultimately also Syrian withdrawal from the country. But as Israeli withdrawal had been made contingent upon Syrian withdrawal, neither seemed likely. Moreover, Syria threatened the renewal of civil strife should Lebanon ratify the treaty [142]. From Damascus's perspective, Israel had achieved what it wanted – a political deal with Beirut, an enfeebled PLO and a broad band of Lebanese territory under direct control. On 5 March 1984, following talks between Asad and Gemayel, Lebanon unilaterally abrogated the agreement.

REPERCUSSIONS OF THE INVASION

In the summer of 1985 Israel decided to withdraw its troops to the security zone. Having had its fingers badly burnt, security for the northern border became the focus of Israel's Lebanon policy. The Lebanon war had tarnished the standing of the Israeli defence establishment and had split Israeli society. Israel had taken six days to reach Beirut in June 1982, laid siege to the city for three months, occupied the Shouf mountains for a year and the western Bekaa and south for three years [107]. Israel's gains were a defunct peace agreement and the evacuation of the PLO, both of which were incommensurate with the heavy Israeli casualties, international condemnation after Sabra and Shatilla, the economic costs of an estimated $1 million a day, and the resumption of attacks against Israel from southern Lebanon. Palestinian nationalism in the West Bank and Gaza Strip also increased. Military gains had clearly not translated into political ones.

The costs of the Lebanon war had severe repercussions on Israeli society. Horrified by massacres of civilians, questionable military results and strategy, and having been 'sold' a limited operation while, all the time, a 'grand plan' had been in the minds of decision-makers, caused outcry in the Israeli population. This clear 'war of choice' rekindled debates in the military establishment on the limits of military force, it questioned the notion of 'purity of arms', and resulted in Israel's first conscientious objectors. The war also provided the peace movement with new life. Peace Now and other groups gained momentous support as well as considerable criticism from a now deeply divided Israeli society. From the Lebanon war onwards, Israel remained split over the issue of negotiations, territorial concessions and security policy.

Within journalistic and academic circles Israel's Lebanon war sparked a debate on the underlying reasons and, ultimately, responsibility. The conventional view holds Defence Minister Ariel Sharon responsible to a large degree and Prime Minister Begin to a more limited degree [122]. The war is seen as the result of Sharon's personal ambitions, thereby absolving the rest of the Israeli decision-making elite. The conventional perspective further maintains that the invasion of Lebanon is an aberration in Israeli foreign and defence policy. This view has been challenged on a number of grounds. First, Sharon, while bearing a significant amount of responsibility, was not solely responsible. Instead the decision-making elite as a whole was responsible and the hawkish direction can be explained through the common phenomenon of 'groupthink'. Secondly, Israel's Lebanon war was not an aberration but the culmination of a long-standing

Lebanon policy since the 1920s, which was based on false premises. Returning to earlier discussions of interventionism or non-interventionism in Israeli foreign policy, Israel's Lebanon policy from the creation of the states of Lebanon and Israel onwards is a clear example of Israeli interventionism [124].

While the war sparked intense debate in Israel, it was used as a stick by Lebanese Muslims to beat the Maronites with. As a result of collaboration with Israel, the Maronites lost their preferential standing. Instead of ruling Lebanon, they now had to defend their very existence [132]. By the end of the civil war in 1990 a sizeable segment of the Christian community had found refuge abroad. Lebanon's dependence upon Syria was formalised through the 1989 Taif Accord and the 1990 Treaty of Brotherhood and Friendship. Syria had emerged in a stronger position than ever before, becoming the arbiter over Lebanon's future.

For the Palestinians changes were no less dramatic. The PLO lost its last border access to Israel with its evacuation to Tunis in 1982. This had the effect of shifting PLO strategy towards a more diplomatic level, while in the long-run returning the struggle to those Palestinians under Israeli occupation in the West Bank and Gaza Strip. So rather than eliminating the influence of the PLO, Palestinian nationalism became stronger, while at the same time, through the shift in strategy, the PLO gained increased international recognition. The link between the two made it unequivocally clear that, ultimately, Israel would have no choice but to negotiate with the PLO.

8 THE *INTIFADA*

The aims of Israel's invasion of Lebanon included destroying not only the PLO's military basis but its political one as well. Operation Peace for Galilee was intended to strike a severe blow at the PLO's international standing and to weaken the budding resistance and nationalism in the West Bank and Gaza Strip. With the evacuation of the PLO from Beirut to Tunis, Israel seemed to have achieved at least one aim of the 1982 invasion. The Palestinian guerrilla movement had lost access to Israel's border. Yet it was exactly the PLO's Lebanon experience which laid the foundation for the 1987 *intifada** uprising in the Israeli occupied territories as well as the PLO's decision to declare an independent Palestinian state with a government in exile. The abandonment by Arab politicians, the Sabra and Shatilla massacres, and the move of the PLO to Tunis, shifted the focus to the West Bank and Gaza Strip, encouraging local politicians. At the same time, the marginalisation of the PLO, now in Tunis, also led to a tactical shift from guerrilla warfare to a diplomatic offensive. Both the PLO's international standing and Palestinian nationalism increased as a result. Thus in the long-run, Israel's determination to remove the Palestinian presence from Lebanon achieved the opposite effect.

THE PLO AFTER 1982

The military defeat of the Palestinian resistance in Lebanon after the siege of Beirut revealed the shortcomings of the PLO's strategy. The notion of armed struggle as the foundation for the establishment of a Palestinian state was called into question [56]. The guerrilla struggle after 1967 and the semi-regularised army developed in South Lebanon in the late-1970s, had been ineffective in liberating Palestine. With the dispersion of PLO forces in nine Arab countries, a plausible military option no longer existed.

The lack of a 'battlefield', however, was not the only problem faced by the resistance movement. Factionalisation and friction dominated Palestinian politics. Arafat's opponents, with Syrian encouragement, condemned him for the defeat and were highly critical of his decision to consider a diplomatic option [131]. The move to Tunis had physically cut off the Palestinian leadership from the bulk of the Palestinian people. The PLO's isolation was further compounded by the lack of support from its Arab brothers, most of whom had been unwilling to accept the PLO after its evacuation from Beirut. 'Having suffered a profound blow as a result of its military defeat in Lebanon, with its cadres and fighters now scattered over a dozen countries, the PLO ran the risk of permanent fragmentation' [136 *p.610*]. Palestinian strategy needed to be reassessed.

The debate within the PLO focused on the future of the resistance movement; the 1982 Reagan peace plan [*Doc. 16*] which called for Palestinian autonomy as outlined in the Camp David Accords; the Fez plan [*Doc. 17*] drawn up at an Arab summit meeting on 9 September 1982, calling for Israeli withdrawal, the dismantling of settlements, a PLO government, compensation for refugees, and a two-state solution; and the possibility of Jordanian–PLO *rapprochement*. Playing his cards cautiously, Arafat embarked upon separate negotiations with the United States and Jordan. 'The initial positions of the Palestinian leader were: yes to the establishment of a Jordanian–Palestinian confederation; but after the establishment of a Palestinian state; no to any delegation of power during the negotiations' [56 *p. 231*].

Yet Arafat received little encouragement for his diplomatic initiative. Opposition within his own ranks was fuelled by Syria, Iraq and Libya. Official Israeli policy remained that the PLO should have no role whatsoever in any negotiations. This position was supported by the Reagan administration, leaving little room for the PLO to manoeuvre. At the same time, the United States pushed for a Jordanian solution for the West Bank, which envisaged Israel giving up territory as well as accepting Palestinian negotiators from the West Bank and Gaza Strip [131]. It was in this context that at the 16th PNC in February 1983, the PLO accepted the Arab Fez plan, and officially refused the Reagan plan, but not the process initiated by the United States. Beyond finding an acceptable negotiating position, 'the true leitmotif of the Council was the affirmation of national unity and the independence of Palestinian decision-making *vis-à-vis* the Arab regimes' [56 *p. 233*]. It was clear that survival had become the most important objective of the PLO post-Lebanon.

While the PLO was searching for a unified position and diplomatic avenues, Israel under its new National Unity Government under the premiership of Shimon Peres sought a settlement with Jordan, to the exclusion of the PLO. The prospects for an Israeli–Jordanian agreement, however, were undermined by Likud encouragement of settlements in the West Bank as well as by Arafat's decision actively to pursue PLO–Jordanian *rapprochement*. Jordan, too, pushed its own interests in the search for an acceptable agreement. 'As the central Arab player in the American design, as well as a pivotal member of the emerging bloc of mainstream Arab states, Jordan would see its political fortunes improve should the peace process go forward' [136 *p. 618*].

On 11 February 1985, an agreement between Jordan and the PLO was signed. The Amman Agreement, or Hussein–Arafat Accord, [*Doc. 19*] called for the establishment of a Palestinian state on the West Bank in confederation with Jordan. It envisaged a complete Israeli withdrawal from the territory, including East Jerusalem, in return for peace. Implicitly this meant the recognition of Israel's right to exist.

This agreement opened the way for negotiations between the Palestinian resistance and the US administration, but fell short of genuine Jordanian–PLO reconciliation. Both Jordan and the PLO saw American approval of their overtures as a way to stop Israeli settlement policy [131]. King Hussein further saw the agreement as a way to protect himself against the challenge from Arab radicalism as well as a possibility of further extending his influence over the West Bank and Gaza Strip [136].

While the PLO and Jordan were discussing the composition of a future joint Palestinian–Jordanian team for eventual peace negotiations, Palestinian radicals attempted completely to derail any possible talks by attacking Israel. This triggered yet another round of Israeli–Palestinian violence. On 25 September 1985, three Israelis were killed in Cyprus. On 1 October, Israel bombed PLO headquarters in Tunis, killing 56 Palestinians and 15 Tunisians. On 7 October, PFLP leader Abu Abbas instigated the hijacking of the Italian liner, the *Achille Lauro*. International outrage over the murder of crippled American Jew Leon Klinghoffer brought all cautious advances towards the PLO to an immediate standstill [99].

These problems were further compounded by the US administration's support of direct Jordanian–Israeli talks, with the result that the US administration displayed a clear lack of interest in the PLO–Jordan initiative. Israel, too, remained obstinate. It was not going to negotiate with the PLO in any form.

By February 1986, the situation had deteriorated to such an extent that when Arafat offered to accept UNSC resolutions 242 and 338 in return for American recognition of the Palestinians' right to self-determination, US President Ronald Reagan refused point-blank. The United States was 'not in favour of an independent Palestinian state'. Reports that King Hussein was secretly making arrangements with Israel for joint-control of the West Bank added to the tension. Then, on 19 February, in the face of the PLO's refusal to endorse UNSC 242, King Hussein decided to abrogate the Jordanian–PLO agreement [136]. Arafat, however, remained determined to pursue a political solution. On 5 September 1986 at the non-aligned summit in Harare, he declared:

> The PLO has done everything in its power to reach a just and equitable solution, preserving the inalienable rights of the Palestinian people as defined in international law, including their right to return, to self-determination and to build their own independent state, with Jerusalem as its capital. We demand that an international conference be held to establish peace in the region as a whole. [56 p. 241]

The PLO remained in an unenviably weak position during 1986 and 1987. Four years of diplomacy had achieved nothing, while Israeli settlement policy continued and Israeli–Palestinian clashes in the Territories increased steadily. The outbreak of the *intifada* in December 1987, however, changed the situation irreversibly. The Jordan option favoured by both Israel and the United States became untenable.

THE *INTIFADA*

On 8 December 1987, an Israeli army transport crashed into a line of Arab cars carrying labourers in Gaza. Four Palestinians were killed and seven injured. Rumours that the accident had in fact been an act of retaliation for an Israeli stabbed to death the previous day in Gaza's main market, spread rapidly, and demonstrations erupted during the funerals of the victims. The demonstrations spread from the Gaza Strip to the West Bank; a Palestinian popular uprising had begun. It provided the Palestinians with an outlet for frustration and anger at Israel's occupation, operations conducted in the name of security, Israel's expanding settlement policy, Israel's control of water resources, and the growing aggressiveness of Jewish settlers. Palestinian men, women and children stood up to Israeli soldiers with a determination not seen before. Israeli politicians, however, refused to accept the source of Palestinian discontent, instead blaming Iran,

Syria and the PLO for the uprising which became known as the *intifada* (shaking off) [99].

Contrary to Israeli perception, the *intifada* had not been instigated by outside powers, but was a spontaneous uprising. It started as a rebellion of the forsaken and forgotten at the bottom of the social heap [123]. 'At its heart, the *intifada* was a rebellion of the poor and the youth, the less-advantaged sectors of the population who organised popular committees that PLO representatives then sought to co-opt under their direction' [131 *p. 297*]. The strategy was one of civil disobedience, restricting itself to stone-throwing, demonstrations and protests. It was aimed at showing the injustice of life under military occupation.

> Palestinians felt they had reached a dead end: they were not living as free human beings and they had no hope for the future. That sense of total blockage internally combined with the sense that no help could be expected from the outside. The PLO was too fragmented and distant, and the Arab states had lost interest. Europe and the Soviet Union lacked leverage and the US was too committed to Israel to comprehend the Palestinian situation, much less broker a satisfactory accord. [81 *p. 4*]

When the *intifada* erupted, the PLO was no less surprised than Israel and the PLO leadership at first was uncertain how to react [86]. Consequently, a political agenda from the PLO leadership in Tunis did not appear until January 1988, after the local Unified National Command (UNC)* had issued its fourteen-point plan. 'The fourteen points were divided between demands for Israeli concessions regarding self-determination; directives for the population on how to retain the pressure through strikes and demonstrations; and a request – directed to the PLO – to include Palestinians from inside the Occupied Territories in the structure of the PNC' [23 *p. 192*]. In response to the local leadership and in an attempt to exert its control over events, the PLO called for the establishment of an independent Palestinian state that would co-exist with Israel. The uprising, it claimed, would continue until the basis for 'real peace' had been reached. The strategy for resistance on the ground was one of widespread civil disobedience. The Palestinian population was urged to sever all connections with the Israeli occupiers by boycotting Israeli goods, by refusing to pay taxes, and by refusing to work for Israelis. This was augmented by general strikes, demonstrations, and flying the prohibited Palestinian flag. Committees were organised and forces were co-ordinated through the UNC, which comprised elements from Fatah, the PFLP, the DFLP* and the Palestine Communist Party. These committees were not only responsible for the *intifada* but also for social services ranging from supplying villages under curfew with food and establishing education programmes to arranging for the care of wounded Palestinians. Islamist parties such as Islamic Jihad and Hamas*, which were only starting to become political players, became progressively involved. Steadfastness, or *sumud**, had become central to the Palestinian strategy [135], and for the first time in history the Palestinian people were unified.

The question is sometimes asked, why it took so long for the *intifada* to erupt. When Israel occupied the West Bank and Gaza Strip in 1967, the Palestinians in the Territories were exchanging one form of foreign control for another. Initially, they seemed even to have benefited. In the 1970s Palestinians under Israeli rule received higher wages than those under Jordanian rule. Jewish settlements were also small in number and isolated from Arab villages at that time. And at that time the PLO still had a credible military strategy. This situation changed in the 1980s. Israel's settlement policy intensified. Between 1977 and 1987 the number of Israeli settlers increased from under 5,000 to more than 60,000, and the number of settlements from 36 to 100 [104]. Israel under the Likud government was 'creating facts on the ground', through a policy of creeping annexation. Not only did the overall number of settlements increase, but they also started to appear right next to Arab villages. The message was unequivocal. In addition, economic recession in Israel led to a decline in the Palestinian standard of living, the situation being particularly bad in the over-populated camps in the Gaza Strip. The PLO was defeated in Lebanon. And, finally, a younger generation of Palestinians had come of age. They lacked the comparative experience of Jordanian rule which their parents had endured, and no longer looked towards Jordan for a solution. They had known nothing but the occupation, with its frustrations and humiliations [47]. Daily contact with Israeli soldiers had ensured that the 'fear factor' was minimal. It was time for the Palestinians to take their future into their own hands.

The emergence of a local leadership within the framework of the *intifada* provided both challenges and opportunities for the PLO [136]. The biggest challenge, by far, however, was the high economic price paid by the population. Many Palestinians who had previously been employed in Israel lost their jobs, and unemployment reached over 50 per cent at times. Small businesses collapsed under the burden of curfews and general strikes. Farmers were unable to reach markets to sell their produce and were often cut off from their fields because of military restrictions.

ISRAELI REACTION

Israeli decision-makers initially expected the protests to die down. Defence Minister Rabin, believing the disturbances were nothing more than 'normal unrest', departed on a trip to the United States. Indeed, it took a month for everyone to realise that the continuing incidents could not be suppressed in routine fashion [104]. Nevertheless, Israeli decision-makers still treated the *intifada* in light of existing policy on Arab protest. The uprising was just another form of 'terrorism' and was accordingly approached by the use of force. New measures were instated with Rabin's policy of 'might, power, and beatings', as an alternative to live ammunition. This was accompanied by the use of tear-gas, mass arrests, torture under detention, and curfews. But none of these measures was able to bring the uprising under control. Rather, it fuelled Palestinian determination, started to stir criticism within Israel, and aroused international outrage. Israel's international and domestic image declined further when, in April 1988, the Israeli cabinet approved the assassination of Khalil al-Wazir (Abu Jihad) in his Tunis home, believing him to be the instigator of the uprising [131]. On 15 April, an Israeli taskforce of four boats and a submarine set out for Tunis. In the early hours of 16 April, two commandos went ashore, entered Abu Jihad's villa and shot him in front of his wife. The Israeli raid, which had taken no longer than five minutes, succeeded only in stopping the latest set of directives to the UNC [23 *p. 194*]. It failed to stop the *intifada* and, much to Israel's chagrin, Abu Jihad's death led to a *rapprochement* between Arafat and Syria [99].

Despite stepping-up its security measures, it was noticeable that Israel did not have an effective overall strategy. The IDF was unable to end the uprising and its operations turned into damage limitation exercises. Israeli forces were unable to occupy 500 Arab villages simultaneously [104]. In addition to military measures, Israel employed administrative measures in an effort to contain the *intifada*. Universities were closed, primary and secondary schools were suspended for lengthy periods of time, dozens of houses were blown up, entire communities were placed under curfew, suspected activists were deported, Arabic-language newspapers were censored, charities were closed, and the transfer of currency into the Territories was restricted [136]. The military and financial costs of keeping the Territories under Israeli control rose dramatically and with them the economic burden on the state. But it was the political costs that really left Israeli decision-makers gasping for breath.

While the uprising did not lead to immediate Palestinian statehood, it had effectively restored the Green Line, threatening Israel's 'historic' claims to the West Bank and Gaza Strip. The notion of Palestinian docility under occupation had been shattered. The separation of the territories was further underscored when, on 31 July 1988, King Hussein relinquished Jordan's claim to the West Bank [*Doc. 20*]. In the wake of Jordan's move, Israeli decision-makers were unsure about their next move. Labour, which had advocated the Jordan option, saw Likud's position strengthened in the run-up to the November general elections.

In the meantime, the PLO and the local Palestinian leadership were making preparations for statehood. Against the background of mounting international and domestic criticism of Israeli efforts to contain the *intifada*, the PNC proclaimed the state of Palestine with Jerusalem as its capital in November 1988 [*Doc. 22*]. By 1989 it had been recognised by more than 100 countries. The PNC also announced its readiness to negotiate with Israel on the basis of UNSC resolutions 242 and 338. This was followed by Arafat's renunciation of terrorism and recognition of Israel in December, opening the way for US–PLO dialogue. Israel, however, conceded little. The Shamir government offered 'elections for autonomy' over unspecified daily affairs and the Palestinians, as predicted, rejected the offer. Violence continued: US State Department statistics estimated that 366 Palestinians had died and more than 20,000 were wounded in the *intifada* by February 1989 [99]. By the end of 1989, 626 Palestinians and 43 Israelis had been killed, 37,439 Palestinians wounded, and an estimated 40,000 arrested [67].

In April 1989, Arafat was elected as the first Palestinian president. Israel, whose international standing was severely damaged by media coverage of armed soldiers beating unarmed women and children, had to act. The role of policing the Territories also had a demoralising effect upon Israeli soldiers. A number of new peace groups emerged and for the first time the Israeli army was faced with a significant number of conscientious objectors to service in the West Bank and Gaza Strip. The left-wing Peace Now movement gained increasing support for its demonstrations [84; 86], while, at the same time, the extreme right was becoming more popular. Israeli proposals for resolving the situation were no less polarised, ranging from full Israeli withdrawal to the expulsion of all Palestinians. Israeli Prime Minister

Shamir's 1989 peace plan emerged in this context as a response to the PLO peace initiative. It called for a halt to the *intifada* and for elections to be held in the Territories. The aim of the elections was to select a Palestinian delegation with which Israel would negotiate in order to establish a self-governing authority in the West Bank and Gaza Strip during an interim period, to be followed by additional negotiations to determine the final status of these territories [136]. The Shamir plan received cautious approval from the United States, but the plan collapsed only weeks later, when US Secretary of State James Baker pushed the notion of land for peace. The Palestinians, too, did not feel the plan offered enough, especially as it did not give a role to the PLO.

Shamir's position of a 'Greater Israel' improved briefly, with the sudden influx of Russian Jews after the collapse of the Soviet Union. He spoke of settling the Russians in the Territories. His ambition, though, ran up against US determination to stop such settlement plans, if necessary through cuts in US aid. While US–Israeli relations were tense over Israel's settlement policy US–PLO relations faltered over the definition of terrorism and the notion of legitimate targets. US President George Bush finally suspended the dialogue with the PLO on 20 June 1990, after a Palestinian raid on a beach near Tel Aviv.

Despite the lack of progress towards a diplomatic solution, and despite the fact that the official position of the Israeli government had not changed, the *intifada* had a clear impact on political thinking in the Jewish state. Israeli politicians and the public alike started to realise that the Palestinian problem was at the core of the Arab–Israeli conflict and that negotiations would, therefore, ultimately have to be with the PLO [136]. The uprising made it clear to the United States and Israel that the Jordan option was dead. At the same time the PLO was forced to abandon its policy of 'constructive ambiguity' [104 *p. 95*]. Above all, the *intifada* put the Palestinian issue back on the international agenda and empowered the Palestinian people.

THE CREATION OF HAMAS

The final development within the context of the *intifada* to be discussed here is the emergence of an Islamist alternative. Israeli intelligence officials had advocated the encouragement of religious groups in the Gaza Strip as a means of counter-balancing the influence of the PLO in the 1970s. 'For the better part of a decade, the Israelis had allowed fundamentalist Muslims to move into positions of power in the religious establishment' [123 *p. 223*]. While no serious rift developed between the PLO and the Islamists, the decline of the PLO after 1982 created a void, and Islamic politics had found a foothold in Gaza.

On 14 December 1987, a new organisation, Hamas (Islamic Resistance Movement), appeared on the political scene. Its first communiqué described itself as a branch of the Muslim Brotherhood and linked itself to a 'chain of *jihad*' through Arab Revolt leader Izz al-Din al-Qassim [84; 99]. Its newly established leadership, including Sheikh Ahmed Yassin and Dr Abd al-Aziz al-Rantisi from the Islamic University of Gaza, reflected its broader social appeal.

With its emergence Hamas not only swallowed up the Muslim Brotherhood, it also became an Islamic alternative to the secular PLO. The movement advocated an Islamist–nationalist doctrine, challenging the PLO's claim to be the sole legitimate representative of the Palestinian people through its religious vision, political and social goals, as well as its communal action [91]. Hamas' goals were the creation of a Palestinian state in all of Palestine based on Islamic principles and Shari'a law, as set out in the Hamas Charter [*Doc. 21*] in August 1988. Article 6, for example, defines the struggle against Israel as one to be 'waged over every inch of Palestine', which it considers to be an inalienable Muslim endowment or *waqf**, while articles 12 and 15 address the sacred duty of every individual Muslim to fight the enemy threatening Muslim land.

The *intifada* brought to the surface both the primacy and urgency of Palestinian activism. Islamist organisations existing prior to the uprising had focused on communal activities. The *intifada* shifted this focus towards political activism and violence against Israel in pursuit of an Islamic state in all of territorial Palestine [91].

Hamas called upon the Palestinian population to co-operate in both violent and non-violent actions. 'The controlled civil revolt, like the continuous decline in the number of directives calling for severance of economic ties with Israel, was evidence that from the very beginning of the *intifada*, Hamas had calculated its strategy on the basis of cost–benefit considerations' [91 *p. 20*].

The PLO's initial response to the emergence of an Islamist alternative was conciliatory, praising its historical record of armed struggle. At the same time, Hamas declared its willingness to work with the PLO on an agreed agenda for the liberation of Palestine, while remaining beyond the authority of the UNC. Indeed, throughout the *intifada* as a whole, Hamas capably demonstrated its flexibility by differentiating between the short-term goal of establishing a Palestinian state in the West Bank and Gaza, and the long-term goal of establishing a Palestinian

Islamic state that would replace Israel [91]. The PLO's conciliatory position had been influenced by the belief that an outright clash with Hamas would destroy the *intifada* [123]. Yet rivalry between the two organisations was evident in the struggles over who would control the strikes.

In spring 1990, the control of the UNC and the PLO's influence were clearly slipping away, and there were armed clashes between Fatah and Hamas. Dissatisfaction with the lack of progress of the uprising led Palestinians to turn towards more radical solutions including Hamas and the PFLP, despite the PLO's argument that Israel had supported the establishment of Hamas in order to weaken the *intifada* [123]. In an attempt to recapture control, Arafat moved closer to the last 'pan-Arab' leader, Saddam Hussein, a move which placed him on the wrong side of the international community only months later when Iraq invaded Kuwait.

9 THE MIDDLE EAST PEACE PROCESS

The collapse of the Soviet Union in 1989 and the consequent end of the Cold War changed the old bipolar world order to a new unipolar, US-led international system. Former Soviet clients in the Middle East, who could no longer rely on Soviet military and economic aid, cautiously re-oriented themselves towards the United States and Europe. At the same time, staunch US allies in the region came under closer scrutiny, often resulting in less uncritical support. These changes were accompanied by a reassessment of US–Israeli relations as well as a US–Arab realignment. This process of reassessment was further hastened by the 1990–91 Gulf War. Indeed, Iraq's invasion of Kuwait on 2 August 1990 brought former Soviet clients such as Syria into an uneasy alliance with the West, while Israel turned from a long-standing strategic asset into a political liability.

THE GULF WAR

On 2 August 1990 Iraq invaded and occupied Kuwait. The invasion served the combined purposes of alleviating Iraq's financial and economic problems after the eight-year-long Iran–Iraq war, avoiding unemployment and discontent from having to demobilise a large standing army, fulfilling long-standing territorial aspirations, and becoming a regional superpower [13]. Following diplomatic moves to deter further aggression and restore Kuwaiti sovereignty, the United States, the European Union, Russia and the Arab League froze both Iraqi and Kuwaiti assets and imposed sanctions upon Iraq. US troops were airlifted to Saudi Arabia and a US-led multinational coalition started to emerge. Yet, despite the military build-up, Iraq assumed that the coalition would not dare to attack [113].

The most immediate effect of the invasion upon the region was that it split the Arab world into those who supported Saddam and those who opposed him. Egypt, Saudi Arabia, Syria, Kuwait, Bahrain,

Qatar, Morocco, Oman and the United Arab Emirates supported the US-led coalition effort against the invasion. Libya, Sudan, Yemen and Jordan were either ambivalent or supported Iraq [104]. There was also no doubt about Palestinian sympathy, especially since the Iraqi Revolutionary Council insisted that any talks on the situation in the Gulf should also address the situation of the Palestinians. Indeed, Saddam Hussein personally suggested that Israel withdraw from the occupied Arab territories in Palestine immediately and unconditionally, along with Syrian withdrawal from Lebanon and Iranian withdrawal from areas of Iraq. Only then would Iraq be willing to discuss the situation in Kuwait [23 *p. 201*]. Such linkage was not surprising as it deflected from Iraq's actions and reflected the closer PLO–Iraqi relationship from 1989 onwards. 'Arafat considered Saddam the region's new strongman and, at the May 1990 Arab summit in Baghdad, helped Iraq's dictator try to crown himself as the Arabs' leader ... Baghdad's missiles and chemical weapons gave Arabs the strength "to achieve liberation from Baghdad to Jerusalem" ' [112 *p. 155*]. In the absence of an Israeli response to Palestinian efforts of conciliation and moderation, Arafat believed that only force could shift Israeli intransigence, and Saddam Hussein appeared to be the means to this end.

Following numerous UN resolutions calling upon Iraq to redeploy troops voluntarily, the deadline for Iraqi withdrawal from Kuwait expired on 15 January 1991. On the night of 16–17 January, the anti-Saddam coalition launched Operation Desert Storm to liberate Kuwait. While the coalition bombed Iraqi positions in Kuwait and Iraq, Saddam Hussein launched Scud missiles against Saudi Arabia and Israel. By targeting Israel, Iraq not only reinforced the linkage already created, but also attempted to provoke Israeli retaliation in order to split the coalition. Israel's decision to opt for restraint was not an easy one. Indeed, much in keeping with past military doctrine, Ariel Sharon argued that 'we should use the air force to attack the missiles in west Iraq, and if there is no choice, we should act by land; and, in the worst case scenario, we should also take our ground forces through Jordan' [23 *p. 204*]. Ultimately, US assurances and the speedy delivery of Patriot missiles convinced Israeli decision-makers that restraint was the better policy.

The Palestinian response was less ambiguous. Support for Saddam Hussein increased with the Scud attacks. For Palestinians, Saddam Hussein was the only Arab leader willing to stand up to the West. 'Moreover, Palestinians contrasted the West's prompt action over Kuwait, where economic interests were strongly engaged, with twenty-five years' inaction over the Occupied Territories' [47 *p. 141*].

Palestinian reaction was to some degree a 'revolt' against the perceived double standard of the West which had reacted quickly and forcefully against Saddam's aggression while tolerating continued Israeli occupation of the West Bank and Gaza Strip [136]. Reports of Palestinians cheering the Iraqi missiles from their rooftops, however, only served to alienate international opinion [99].

The allied offensive ended on 28 February, leaving Iraq's armed forces scattered and destroyed. The Gulf War revealed the divisions in the Arab world. Sympathy for the Palestinian cause had been weakened and resulted in a financial crisis for the PLO because Arab Gulf support was withdrawn. But Israel, too, had been affected. The Scud attacks had made it very clear that the territory of the West Bank was not always able to enhance security, and that due to the hostile population the risks of additional territory were greater than its benefits [123]. Israel had also become a liability for the United States. And, above all, the Gulf War made it clear that regional stability had to be put at the top of the international agenda. It is therefore not surprising that by the end of the war two issues needed to be addressed: Iraq's potential to threaten the region, and the instability caused by the Arab–Israeli conflict.

THE MADRID CONFERENCE AND FRAMEWORK FOR PEACE

The peace process in the Middle East was officially initiated with a letter of invitation [*Doc. 23*] to the US–Russian co-sponsored Madrid conference. It followed US Secretary of State James Baker's extensive shuttles to the Middle East between March and October, in which he put his peace plan to Arab and Israeli leaders. According to Baker, 'the idea was to give both the Arabs and the Israelis what they needed. The Arabs wanted an international conference supervised by other countries, the Israelis wanted face-to-face negotiations with their Arab neighbours' [23 p. 206]. So on 30 October, Israel, for the first time, sat down with Syria, Lebanon and Jordan, the delegation for Jordan being a joint Palestinian–Jordanian one. 'The tacit understanding between all the Arab participants had been that the accord with Israel would be achieved by them as a group' [139 p. 4].

While the parties invited to the conference did not engage with each other on a substantive level, a framework for negotiations was nevertheless constructed. The Madrid framework divided the talks into bilateral and multilateral tracks. The bilateral track aimed at achieving separate peace treaties between Israel and its Arab neighbours

Syria, Lebanon, Jordan and the Palestinians. The multilateral track was designed to resolve issues affecting the region as a whole, promoting peace, stability and co-operation. The working groups on water, the environment, arms control, refugees, and economic development, which were set up within this track, include not only delegates from the Middle East but also representatives from the international community.

After the opening conference the negotiations moved to Washington where they soon reached a stalemate. The problems became evident when the Israeli delegation failed to turn up for the negotiations during the first week in the belief that 'the safest way to avoid concessions was to stay at home' [72 *p. 85*]. Once the delegation did arrive, Israel remained steadfast in its stipulation not to include the PLO. At the same time Palestinian representatives of the Jordanian delegation were limited by the PLO refusal to give them decision-making powers [139]. The backdrop of continued Israeli settlement policy in the Occupied Territories and the deterioration of Israeli Prime Minister Itzhak Shamir's relations with the United States made progress virtually impossible.

THE OSLO PROCESS AND ISRAELI–PALESTINIAN NEGOTIATIONS

The June 1992 election victory of Labour in Israel provided a new environment for the Middle East peace process [43]. This environment was further aided by the unintended 'benign neglect' shown during the first months of the Clinton administration, which created the space for Norwegian mediation [141]. Unofficial Israeli–Palestinian talks started on two separate avenues: Oslo and London. These talks provided both sides with the possibility of exploring each other's positions without recognition, commitment, or indeed violating Israeli law under which meetings with the PLO were illegal. The Oslo process began to crystallise towards the end of the year, when the Knesset passed a bill lifting restrictions on contacts with the PLO for private individuals. The first round of pre-negotiations in Norway followed on 20–22 January 1993. Norway considered itself to be an appropriate facilitator for Israeli–Palestinian talks as it did not have any major interests in the Middle East and was on good terms with both Israel and the Palestinians. Three main ideas were agreed upon by PLO negotiator Abu Alaa and Israeli academic Yair Hirschfeld. There would be Israeli withdrawal from Gaza, gradual devolution of economic power to the Palestinians, and international economic assistance.

Unofficial talks were further helped by the fact that both Israelis and Palestinians had agreed to avoid delving into historic grievances.

At the same time, Israeli–Palestinian negotiations in Washington moved at a snail's pace. Even agreeing to an agenda for the negotiations proved to be a nightmare. Talks broke down completely in December 1992, when Israel deported 415 Palestinian Islamists to South Lebanon. While the PLO may have secretly approved of the removal of some its rivals, it had publicly to condemn Israeli action and felt compelled to boycott the negotiations. The stalemate in Washington focused minds in Oslo and, ultimately, resulted in Rabin's decision to upgrade the Oslo process and replace Israeli academics with government negotiators. The Declaration of Principles (DOP)* [*Doc. 24*] was drafted, redrafted and amended throughout spring and summer 1993. Aspects of jurisdiction, security and Jerusalem remained a sticking point, as did the issue of mutual recognition.

On 30 August 1993, Rabin presented the DOP to the cabinet for approval. On 9 September, under the auspices of Norwegian Foreign Minister Johann Jorgen Holst, Arafat and Rabin exchanged letters of mutual recognition [47]. On 13 September 1993, the Israeli–Palestinian DOP (also known as the Oslo Accords) was signed on the White House lawn in Washington. The Declaration outlined the arrangements for interim self-government, early empowerment for Palestinians in the West Bank, as well as elections of a Palestinian council. Permanent status negotiations were scheduled to begin no later than three years following the DOP, with agreement to take effect after the fifth year of the interim period. The DOP did not, however, find approval from all Palestinians. For example, Palestinian negotiator Hanan Ashrawi pointed out that 'it was obvious that the people who wrote the document didn't live under occupation because a freeze on all settlements wasn't included nor was the release of prisoners, which are the two main issues that would have given the document credibility throughout the Occupied Territories' [*139 p. 245*]. The agreement, nevertheless, was of historic significance. It gave each party the recognition it had sought from the other and confirmed before the world that there is nothing about the essence of either Zionism or Palestinian nationalism that makes conflict resolution impossible [136].

The DOP was followed by the Cairo Agreement on 4 May 1994, which included provisions for Israeli military withdrawal, the transfer of authority from the Israeli Civil Administration to the Palestinian Authority, a Palestinian police force, and relations between Israel and the Palestinian Authority [104]. Further progress was made on 28 September 1995, with the Israeli–Palestinian Interim Agreement on the West Bank and Gaza Strip, which aimed at broadening Palestinian autonomy, but also addressed security, elections, economic relations and the release of prisoners.

Palestinian elections were scheduled for 20 January 1996. Arafat received more than 90 per cent of the vote on a voter turnout of 68.46 per cent in the West Bank and 80 per cent in Gaza. The new Palestinian council consisted of 50 members, including four women and six Christians. The elections provided the Palestinian Authority with the required legitimacy. The stability provided by the elections, however, was not able to counter-balance the instability which the assassination of Israeli Prime Minister Rabin on 4 November 1995 had caused. A shocked and deeply divided Israeli society took a collective step back from the peace process. The subsequent election campaign was characterised by insecurity and an increase in Hamas violence. Both were reflected in the victory of a more hard-line Likud government headed by Benjamin Netanyahu. Thus the assassination of Rabin proved to be a turning point, marked by a degree of Israeli disengagement from the peace process.

Against the background of months of stagnation which followed, the Hebron Agreement of January 1997 was hailed as a crucial breakthrough for the deadlocked Israeli–Palestinian negotiations. The Agreement called for the Israeli redeployment from Hebron within ten days and the assumption of responsibility by Palestinian police henceforth. Both sides further committed themselves to the prevention of terrorism with a number of specific provisions of joint security measures. Civil powers and responsibilities with the exception of those relating to Israelis and their property were also to be transferred to the Palestinian side. Israeli responsibilities consisted of further redeployment and the release of Palestinian prisoners. Palestinian responsibilities were the revising of the Palestinian National Charter, and preventing violence.

PEACE WITH JORDAN

The obvious success story in the bilateral strand has been the 1994 Jordanian–Israeli peace agreement. This agreement was concluded without any of the problems plaguing the Israeli–Palestinian negotiations. For one thing, Israel and Jordan did not have a significant territorial dispute; with a few minor adjustments the border between the two states was upheld and recognised. Moreover, there had always been rather amicable but unofficial relations between the two states dating back to the mandate period. While the Israeli–Palestinian relationship may be described as one of extreme distrust and insecurity, trust and a comparative absence of violence had existed in Israeli–Jordanian relations since 1967.

Crucial to the speedy conclusion of the agreement was the fact that Israel and the Palestinians had already signed the 1993 Oslo Accords which cleared the path for Jordanian political moves [43; 104]. Thus, in essence, the Jordanian–Israeli agreement was an official recognition of an already existing situation of non-belligerence – a legal sanction for an inevitable process of normalisation.

The common agenda for the peace treaty was agreed to on 14 September 1993 and consisted of the issues of security, water, refugees and borders. On 25 July 1994, King Hussein and Prime Minister Rabin had their first public meeting, which resulted in the Washington Declaration. The Declaration stated that the 'state of belligerency between Jordan and Israel was terminated', that both states agreed to pursue peace on the basis of UNSC resolutions 242 and 338, and that Israel would respect 'the special role of the Hashemite Kingdom over Muslim holy shrines'. Direct telephone links, joint electricity grids, new border crossings, as well as co-operation on combating crime and drugs smuggling followed. On 26 October 1994 the Jordanian–Israeli Peace Treaty [*Doc. 25*] was signed.

The process of normalisation of relations between Israel and Jordan has focused on additional bilateral agreements in the areas of tourism, environmental co-operation, trade, police co-operation, and agriculture. Joint projects on energy and water have further cemented relations. Yet complete normalisation will remain elusive until psychological barriers within the populations have been dismantled, and, most importantly, a satisfactory outcome of Israeli–Palestinian talks has been achieved.

NEGOTIATIONS WITH SYRIA AND LEBANON

Israeli negotiations with Syria and, by extension, Lebanon have been the most problematic. Syria's president Hafez al-Asad has built his career upon placing Syria at the heart of the Arab–Israeli conflict. Syria's military capabilities were the crucial factor, which made this economically and politically weak country into a regional power. A move from conflict to normalisation of relations will no doubt lead to a marginalisation of Syria. Indeed, this marginalisation has already begun with the opening of Israeli–Jordanian relations, the Clinton administration's mobilisation of international opinion against terrorism with the 1995 Sharm al-Sheikh summit, the new Israeli–Turkish strategic relationship announced in February 1996, and Israel's May

1996 Operation Grapes of Wrath for which the United States is believed to have given its approval. Despite Asad's concessions to peace which included allowing Syrian Jews to leave the country, cleaning up the drug traffic in the Beqaa Valley, and an appearance of the Syrian Foreign Minister Faruq al-Shara on Israeli television, the United States and Israel still seek to portray Syria as a pariah state along with Iraq and Iran. Netanyahu's 'letting Syria stew' approach only confirms this perception.

It is thus no surprise that Asad has been more than reluctant to engage in any substantive peace negotiations with Israel, insisting that Israel gives an undertaking to return the Golan Heights before commencing the talks. The slight movement that has been made was primarily motivated by Syria's need to have better relations with the United States after the loss of its main supporter, the Soviet Union. Moreover, the Syrian troop presence in Lebanon has ensured that Lebanon will also stay out of the peace process until Asad is ready for accommodation. With Syria being the only credible military power that can effectively disarm and dissolve Hizbollah*, Asad is able to use his non-interference with Hizbollah activity against Israel as a lever in the peace process. Thus Syria, like Israel, is able to keep South Lebanon destabilised for its own political ends.

Unlike Syria, Lebanon could benefit greatly from peace in the region. Since the end of its 15-year civil war, Beirut has slowly been re-emerging as a financial and business centre. Normalisation of relations – of course only after the issue of South Lebanon has been satisfactorily resolved – would position Lebanon at the heart of the Middle Eastern banking, business, service and computing sectors, along with Israel and Jordan. One point that should not be overlooked is that Lebanon, through its central position, could, with a little imagination and a lot of goodwill, provide Syria with the solution to its marginalisation.

The fear of marginalisation, which has led Syria to adopt a reluctant negotiating strategy, has also featured centrally in Egypt. Egypt, as the first Arab state to sign a peace treaty with Israel (in 1979), has played the role of facilitator since 1991. While Egypt's commitment to furthering regional peace is unquestionable, it is unlikely that the country will greatly benefit from a new regional order. As a state, that is economically weak and has its fair share of domestic problems, it is more than likely that Egypt too will be pushed to the margins of the developing business relations. Egypt will neither be able to compete in the financial/business sector with Israel, Jordan and Lebanon, nor with the Gulf Emirates. It is also unlikely to be able to compete with

Morocco, Tunisia or even Algeria, which are emerging as key players in integrating the Middle East with European markets. To what extent this fear of marginalisation has influenced Egypt in its role of facilitator is open to speculation, but it should certainly not be disregarded completely.

OBSTACLES TO NEGOTIATIONS

From the outset of the negotiations there have been a number of obstacles: the fate of Jewish settlements in the West Bank and Gaza Strip, the status of Jerusalem, the release of prisoners, violence by extremists, and the different perceptions of the time-frame for negotiations as well as the scale of concessions.

Militant nationalists, both Israeli and Palestinian, have opposed the peace process from the beginning. As signs of progress became evident, their determination to sabotage the negotiations also increased. Ultra-nationalist Jewish settlers vowed never to abandon their homes in the West Bank and to fight anyone who tried to move them [104]. They staged demonstrations, blocked roads, assaulted Palestinians and destroyed Arab property.

Palestinian attempts to disrupt the process originated from the rejectionist PFLP and DFLP, as well as Islamist Hamas. Hamas was particularly successful at creating an atmosphere of terror, which made negotiations difficult, if not impossible. Attacks on Israeli soldiers and civilians as well as on Palestinian supporters of the peace process were increasing, culminating in suicide bombings in the heart of Israel.

Israeli settlement policy also remained an obstacle, especially with Likud's expansionist agenda following the 1996 elections. The government decision to proceed with the Har Homa/Abu Ghneim settlement following the 1997 Hebron Agreement was a clear attempt to stall the impending final status talks, while also signalling a no-compromise position on Jerusalem, Jewish settlement policy and Palestinian statehood. This points to the much larger problem that Israel continues to believe it can 'deal with a Palestinian entity, which will somehow be drawn into a political and economic framework' with Israel and Jordan, but that this entity will not be a state [72].

Another obstacle has been the conflicting perceptions of the time-frame of this peace process. In simple terms, many of Israel's actions have been directed at buying time. In Israel, the peace process is generally perceived as proceeding at too fast a pace. Territory is being given away, while no tangible improvement in the security of Israeli citizens seems to have been gained in return. The electorate's shift from Likud to Labour and back to Likud reflects this insecurity at a popular level. Conversely, for the Palestinian National Authority (PNA)* and the Palestinian people, the negotiations have been progressing too slowly. Even after several accords and protocols following the Madrid conference, Arafat is still unable to point to more than limited autonomy, and is forced to tread a fine line between Israeli demands and challenge from within.

Further problems underlying the process stem from the respective status of the leaders within their own electorates on the one hand and in their underlying motivations on the other. Israeli Prime Minister Yitzhak Rabin's assassination in November 1995 revealed the deep divisions in Israeli society which revolved around the issues of security and territory. Rabin had been able to overcome these cleavages through his strong leadership personality. His successor Shimon Peres, in comparison, could not carry a popular vote in an atmosphere of public fear and anger resulting from Hamas suicide bombings in early 1996. Netanyahu and his campaign to stop further concessions to the Palestinians only had marginally more popular support. This in essence means that the backing for Netanyahu's initial anti-peace process platform was as tenuous as the backing for Peres' pro-peace process platform. In that sense Netanyahu was as much constrained by the opinion of the Israeli people as Peres had been.

Palestinian President Yasser Arafat's position is no stronger, with challenges from the Islamic opposition. Palestinian elections in January 1996 legitimised his leadership, but the delays in the Palestinian–Israeli negotiations and Arafat's consequent inability to deliver tangible results to the Palestinian people undermined his position. These domestic constraints on both sides were exacerbated by continued distrust and the perception that purposes and motives other than peacemaking – such as the desire to elicit US support and sympathy – were the reason for the negotiators' presence at the bargaining table.

PART THREE: ASSESSMENT

10 TOWARDS CONFLICT RESOLUTION

After more than four decades of Arab–Israeli conflict and seven decades of Jewish–Arab violence, the conflict appeared to have reached a new phase in 1991. Differences would no longer be settled through military force but by diplomatic means. The preamble of the 1993 Declaration of Principles ambitiously stated that it was time for Israelis and Palestinians 'to put an end to decades of confrontation and conflict, recognise their mutual legitimate political rights, and strive to live in peaceful coexistence and mutual dignity and security to achieve a just, lasting and comprehensive peace settlement and historic reconciliation' [Doc. 24]. Peace, however, remains elusive.

The Arab–Israeli conflict emerged as one of competing nationalisms laying claim to the same territory – Palestine. Jewish immigration to Palestine beginning at the turn of the century placed Zionists and local Arabs in direct competition with each other. Increased Jewish immigration, land acquisition and institution-building became the focus of the early part of the conflict. British mandate policy from 1922 to 1948 exacerbated inter-communal tensions further, as it was perceived by both Jews and Arabs to be biased in favour of the other. Dissatisfaction with British rule as well as mutual suspicion and fear increasingly led to the use of violence for political ends, while zero-sum* perceptions of the conflict resulted in the belief that coexistence was impossible.

From the turn of the century until the end of the British mandate the conflict was predominantly a Zionist–Palestinian one. There was, however, international influence on the conflict through British and, later, US policy, Arab support during the Arab Revolt and against the UN partition resolution, but also Arab competition with regards to nation- and state-building. With the expiry of the British mandate, the declaration of the state of Israel, and the subsequent attacks by Egypt, Jordan, Syria, Lebanon and Iraq, the conflict turned from a civil war into an inter-state war.

The 1948 war set the parameters of the conflict for the next four decades. The Palestinians were displaced, dispersed and marginalised. They were used as a rhetorical tool for Arab leaders in their competition for regional hegemony. They were controlled politically and militarily to prevent their presence from destabilising states and regions. Yet the resolution of the Palestinian refugee problem remained at the top of the Arab negotiating agenda, posing an obstacle to accommodation with Israel. From an Israeli point of view the cost of peace, if it meant Palestinian repatriation, was too high.

The war also left the issues of territory and security unsatisfactorily resolved. Israel had increased its territory, on the one hand gaining relative security, while on the other hand confirming Arab suspicions of an Israeli expansionist agenda. In the absence of peace, however, Israel could not achieve real security and thus turned into a garrison state. The Arab refusal to recognise Israel's right to exist and the Arab boycott further increased Israel's perception of isolation.

The final issue raised by the 1948 war was that of the city of Jerusalem. Jerusalem was divided as a result of the war, the western part falling under Israeli control and the eastern part under Jordanian control. The partition of the city and the fact that the main Jewish holy sites were inaccessible gave rise to the Israeli aspiration for a united Jerusalem as the capital of the Jewish state.

The next four Arab–Israeli wars did not change the parameters of the conflict significantly. The 1956 Suez crisis increased Israel's military standing and consequently its security, but also led to Egypt's emergence as leader of the Arab world. The introduction of the Cold War framework led to a polarisation of the region, further complicating the search for peace.

The 1967 war boosted the Israeli position through its resounding victory and territorial gains. This, however, only resulted in a hardening of the position of its Arab neighbours who could not possibly negotiate from such a position of asymmetry and achieve a fair compromise, which would have to include the Palestinians as well. The 1967 war added importance to the territorial dimension of the conflict, with Israeli control now extending over the West Bank, Gaza Strip, Golan Heights and Sinai peninsula. The occupation of that territory led to the emergence of an Israeli right-wing territorial maximalist agenda pursued by settlement. The war also led to the emergence of an independent Palestinian national movement, which emancipated itself from the Arab states that had lost the war. This led to the first post-1948 Palestinian–Israeli confrontations within the Occupied Territories. Thus the 1967 war brought the Palestinians onto the Israeli and international agendas.

The 1973 war resulted in one major change: the destruction of Israel's invincibility through the Arab surprise attack. Egypt's early successes in particular levelled the playing-field to such an extent that Egypt felt it could enter negotiations and achieve a fair deal. The 1979 Israeli–Egyptian peace agreement removed the Egyptian front from the Arab–Israeli conflict. The Palestinian refugee situation, Israel's control over the West Bank and Gaza Strip, and Israel's overall security, however, remained unresolved.

The 1982 Lebanon war set in motion a number of developments which, in the long-run, served to create conditions conducive to negotiation ten years later. The evacuation of the PLO from Beirut to Tunis deprived the Palestinian resistance of its last border with Israel, thereby strengthening the diplomatic option. For Israel, the failure to achieve its aims signalled unequivocally that a resolution to the Arab–Israeli conflict and the Palestinian problem could not be achieved by military force.

The Arab–Israeli conflict as a whole thus set the parameters for negotiations. As in many other conflicts, the issues that needed to be addressed in the Arab–Israeli conflict resolution process were quite clear. For Israel this meant recognition, legitimacy and security, while the Arab states wanted a just solution to the Palestinian refugee problem, return of territory, and assurances that Israel would not dominate the region politically, militarily or economically. The Palestinians wanted self-determination and statehood. Underlying issues which also needed to be dealt with included Israeli settlements, political violence, prisoners, the status of Jerusalem, and water. All of these issues can be found in the current peace negotiations and some, such as recognition of the state of Israel, have already been dealt with while others, such as Palestinian statehood, security for Israel, and the territorial question have not been satisfactorily addressed.

While all parties to the conflict knew the broad parameters of negotiations, the obstacles to negotiations seemed insurmountable: seven decades of Jewish–Arab relations riddled with mistrust, broken promises, violence, hatred and almost mutually exclusive interpretations of history. The psychological gap between the parties led to an absence of official and direct negotiations during the conflict. This did not, however, mean that contact between the protagonists was absent. Evidence of secret yet unsuccessful negotiations riddles Arab–Israeli history, but Israel and its Arab neighbours were unable and unwilling to make the necessary concessions required for peace.

The search for Arab–Israeli peace since 1948 makes it clear that the conditions may not always have been conducive for negotiations. Suitable conditions for achieving a lasting peace and stability include:

symmetry between negotiating partners; the recognition that the conflict cannot be resolved through military means; acceptable mediators or facilitators; and a window of opportunity often resulting from a change in the conflict environment.

Asymmetry of power and legitimacy between negotiating partners is particularly obvious when looking at Israel and the Palestinians. Israel, having gained statehood in 1948, proceeded to become a regional superpower through its military victories. The Palestinians, as a non-state actor, were dispersed, displaced and subjected to Arab attempts to control them as well as to Israeli efforts to marginalise them. The weakness of the Palestinians defined their 'national liberation' as 'a struggle for attention, redress, and legitimacy, inseparably interwoven with a struggle for the power to pursue those ends' [146 *p.* 7]. Recognition of the PLO as the sole legitimate representative became a central issue of the conflict, comprising one dimension against the Israeli state and another dimension against the regional and international environment of the conflict.

Asymmetry also existed on the inter-state Arab–Israeli level. For instance, after the 1967 Six Day War, Israel's victory was so resounding that the gap between Israel's power and the Arab states' powerlessness made the conditions unsuitable for negotiations. However, the Arab and especially Egyptian success during the first week of the 1973 war, narrowed the gap to such an extent that it paved the way for the 1979 Israeli–Egyptian peace.

Yet symmetry alone does not guarantee successful negotiations. The recognition that a conflict cannot be resolved through military means, effectively a stalemate, is also required as a condition for negotiation and compromise. The Egyptian–Israeli peace was based on such premises. Both Israel and Egypt were aware that war would not lead to a complete destruction of the other, while an absence of war, under the right circumstances, would lead to numerous benefits, many of which were indirectly related to the negotiations, such as reducing the defence burden or receiving US aid.

The Israeli–Syrian relationship remains the only one in which both sides still resort to a military option, and then only on Lebanese territory. Israel continues to exert influence through the security zone as well as by periodic raids against Hizbollah. Similarly, Syria continues to tolerate if not encourage Hizbollah strikes against Israel. A stalemate may have been reached in the conventional sense, but the costs of the stalemate are predominantly borne by Lebanon.

Mediators have played a prominent role in all Arab–Israeli agreements, starting with the 1949 armistices. The lack of recognition of

Israel by the Arab states and of the PLO by Israel posed an obstacle to direct negotiations. Third-party mediators thus served the function, initially, of communicators and later of manipulators and formulators [145]. Mediators such as the Americans during the Camp David Accords and also in the on-going Middle East Peace Process were thus in a position to put forward their own ideas about possible outcomes and were able to use leverage over various negotiating partners to provide threats or incentives. US leverage was particularly clear at the outset of the current negotiations when threats and incentives forced the reluctant negotiating partners to Madrid, when a window of opportunity emerged as a result of regional and international changes in 1991. The end of the Cold War and the instability triggered by the Gulf War provided the need for a regional settlement.

As a whole, both the Arab–Israeli conflict and the negotiating experience have been characterised by a refusal to scale back maximum demands, to prioritise objectives, and by a lack of willingness to compromise. However, the zero-sum approach does not necessarily reflect a genuine incompatibility of the two sides' goals; rather, that their underlying aims were often something other than a negotiated settlement. For instance, the 1983 Israeli–Lebanese negotiations made it very clear that Lebanon was not interested in peace with Israel but did want to improve its relations with the United States.

The pattern that emerges is one of entrenched positions, dubious motives, poor timing, uninspired leadership and psychological obstacles. It was first broken in 1978 with the Camp David Accords, suggesting that negotiations under the right conditions could be successful. The 1994 Jordanian–Israeli peace treaty as well as Oslo I, Cairo, Oslo II, and the Hebron Agreement are further steps in that direction.

Up to the time of writing, though, Arab–Israeli violence continues, emanating both from parties within the negotiations and from those who are firmly situated outside that framework. As violence is still perceived to be the only leverage that the Palestinians, Syria, and indeed Israel have, violence will continue. It has become as much part of the dynamics as the political posturing and the dialogue. While violence may mean a setback to specific negotiations, within the broader history of the conflict it has not been able completely to stifle the search for peace, however elusive that appears to be.

PART FOUR: DOCUMENTS

DOCUMENT 1 ## FROM THE HUSSEIN–MCMAHON CORRESPONDENCE

The Hussein–McMahon Correspondence is a series of letters exchanged between the British High Commissioner in Egypt, Sir Henry McMahon, and the Amir of Mecca, Sharif Hussein, in 1915–16. The British pledge to support Arab independence in the area, which the Arabs maintain included Palestine, is contained in these letters.

Letter from McMahon to Sharif Hussein   24 October 1915

... it is with great pleasure that I communicate to you on their (HMG) behalf the following statement, which I am confident you will receive with satisfaction:

The two districts of Mersina and Alexandretta and portions of Syria lying to the west of the districts of Damascus, Homs, Hama and Aleppò cannot be said to be purely Arab, and should be excluded from the limits demanded.

With the above modification, and without prejudice to our existing treaties with Arab chiefs, we accept those limits.

As for the regions lying within those frontiers wherein Great Britain is free to act without detriment to the interests of her ally, France, I am empowered in the name of the Government of Great Britain to give the following assurance and make the following reply to your letter:

(1) Subject to the above modifications, Great Britain is prepared to recognise and support the independence of the Arabs in all regions within the limits demanded by the Sharif of Mecca.

(2) Great Britain will guarantee the Holy Places against all external aggression and will recognise their inviolability.

Bernard Reich (ed.), *Arab–Israeli Conflict and Conciliation: A Documentary History*, Praeger, 1995, pp. 19–25.

DOCUMENT 2   THE BALFOUR DECLARATION
2 NOVEMBER 1917

The Balfour Declaration is a letter from Foreign Secretary Arthur Balfour to British Zionist leader Lord Rothschild, supporting the Zionist project in Palestine.

His Majesty's Government view with favour the establishment in Palestine of a national home for the Jewish people, and will use their best endeavours to facilitate the achievement of this object, it being clearly understood that nothing shall be done which may prejudice the civil and religious rights of existing non-Jewish communities in Palestine, or the rights and political status enjoyed by Jews in any other country.

Reich, p. 29

DOCUMENT 3   FROM THE SYKES–PICOT AGREEMENT

The Sykes–Picot Agreement was negotiated between Sir Mark Sykes and Georges Picot in January 1916 and defines areas of British and French interests in the territory of the disintegrating Ottoman Empire.

Letter from Sir Edward Gray to Paul Cambon   15 May 1916
1. That France and Great Britain are prepared to recognise and protect an independent Arab State or a Confederation of Arab States in the areas (A) and (B) marked on the annexed map, under the suzerainty of an Arab chief. That in area (A) France, and in area (B) Great Britain, shall have priority of right of enterprise and local loans. That in area (A) France, and in area (B) Great Britain, shall alone supply advisers or foreign functionaries at the request of the Arab State or Confederation of States.
2. That in the blue area France, and in the red area Great Britain, shall be allowed to establish such direct or indirect administration or control as they desire and as they may think fit to arrange with the Arab State or Confederation of States.
3. That in the brown area there shall be established an international administration, the form of which is to be decided upon after consultation with Russia, and subsequently in consultation with the other Allies, and the representatives of the Shareef of Mecca.

Reich, p. 27

DOCUMENT 4   FROM THE RECOMMENDATIONS OF THE
             PEEL COMMISSION JULY 1937

In 1936 a Royal Commission, headed by Lord Peel, was appointed to investigate the cause of the Arab riots. Its report was published in July 1937 and introduced the notion of partition.

... An irrepressible conflict has arisen between the two national communities within the narrow bounds of one small country. About 1,000,000 Arabs are in strife, open or latent, with some 400,000 Jews. There is no common ground between them. The Arab community is predominantly Asiatic in character, the Jewish community predominantly European. They differ in religion and in language. Their cultural and social life, their ways of thought and conduct, are as incompatible as their national aspirations. These last are the greatest bar to peace. Arabs and Jews might possibly learn to live together in Palestine if they would make a genuine effort to reconcile and combine their national ideals and so build up in time a joint or dual nationality. But this they cannot do. The War and its sequel have inspired all Arabs with the hope of reviving in a free and united Arab world the traditions of the Arab golden age. The Jews similarly are inspired by their historic past. They mean to show what the Jewish nation can achieve when restored to the land of its birth. National assimilation between Arabs and Jews is thus ruled out. In the Arab picture the Jews could only occupy the place they occupied in Arab Egypt or Arab Spain. The Arabs would be as much outside the Jewish picture as the Canaanites in the old land of Israel. The National Home, as we have said before, cannot be half-national. In these circumstances to maintain that Palestinian citizenship has any moral meaning is a mischievous pretence. Neither Arab nor Jew has any sense of service to a single state. ...

Laqueur, [77], pp. 56–8.

DOCUMENT 5   FROM THE MACDONALD WHITE PAPER
                                      17 MAY 1939

The MacDonald White Paper marked the shift of British Palestine policy in a pro-Arab direction. By limiting Jewish immigration and land purchases the British sought to end the Arab Revolt in light of emerging war in Europe.

His Majesty's Government are convinced that in the interests of the peace and well-being of the whole people of Palestine a clear definition of policy and objectives is essential. ... It has therefore been necessary for His Majesty's Government to devise an alternative policy, which will, consistently with their obligations to Arabs and Jews, meet the need of the situation in Palestine. Their views and proposals are set forth below under the three heads, (I) The Constitution, (II) Immigration, and (III) Land.

I. – The Constitution

... His Majesty's Government believe that the framers of the Mandate in which the Balfour Declaration was embodied could not have intended that Palestine should be converted into a Jewish State against the will of the Arab population of the country. ...

II. – Immigtation

... If immigration has an adverse effect on the economic position in the country, it should clearly be restricted; and equally, if it has a seriously damaging effect on the political position in the country, that is a factor that should not be ignored. Although it is not difficult to contend that the large number of Jewish immigrants who have been admitted so far have been absorbed economically, the fear of the Arabs that this influx will continue indefinitely until the Jewish population is in a position to dominate them has produced consequences which are extremely grave for Jews and Arabs alike and for the peace and prosperity of Palestine. ...

(1) Jewish immigration during the next five years will be at a rate which, if economic absorptive capacity permits, will bring the Jewish population up to approximately one-third of the total population ...

(2) The existing machinery for ascertaining economic absorptive capacity will be retained, and the High Commissioner will have the ultimate responsibility for deciding the limits of economic capacity. Before each periodic decision is taken, Jewish and Arab representatives will be consulted.

(3) After the period of five years no further immigration will be permitted unless the Arabs of Palestine are prepared to acquiesce in it.

(4) His Majesty's Government are determined to check illegal immigration, and further preventive measures are being adopted. The numbers of any Jewish illegal immigrants who, despite these measures, may succeed in coming into the country and cannot be deported will be deducted from the yearly quotas. ...

III. – Land

... The Reports of several Commissions have indicated that, owing to the natural growth of the Arab population and the steady sale in recent years of Arab land to Jews, there is now in certain areas no room for further transfers of Arab land, whilst in some other areas such transfers of land must be restricted if Arab cultivators are to maintain their existing standard of life and a considerable landless Arab population is not soon to be created. In these circumstances, the High Commissioner will be given general powers to prohibit and regulate transfers of land. ...

Laqueur, [77], pp. 64–75.

DOCUMENT 6 **PLAN D** **10 MARCH 1948**

Plan D or Dalet has become one of the most controversial documents of the 1948 war. Israelis have portrayed it as a set of defensive military measures, while Palestinians see it as proof of a systematic strategy of ethnic cleansing.

I. Introduction

A. The purpose conveyed in this program is domination over the area of the Jewish state and the protection of its borders, as well as of the blocs of Jewish settlement and population outside its borders, against a regular, semi-regular, or small enemy – operating from bases either outside or within the territory of the state.

B. This Plan is based upon three Plans which preceded it, namely:
   a)   Plan B, September 1945
   b)   Plan of May 1946
   c)   The Joshua Plan – 1948

C. Concerning the above-mentioned Plans: the first and second were intended for the first stage of the disturbances, within the country; while the third was intended for the event of invasion by regular forces from neighbouring countries; the purpose of Plan D is to complement the three preceding Plans regarding those matters in which they are deficient and to adapt them to the projected situation likely to come about upon the conclusion of British rule over the country.

II. Basic Assumptions

The Plan is based upon the following assumptions:

A.   The Enemy

1. Projected Composition of Forces
   – A semi-regular force of liberation of the Arab League, acting from bases which it has seized thus far, or which it will seize in the future.
   – The regular forces of the neighbouring countries which will invade across the borders or will act from bases within the country (the Arab Legion).
   – Small local forces operating from bases within the country and across the borders of the Hebrew state. All three of these forces will act simultaneously, following – with tactical coordination – a joint operative program more or less strictly.

2. Projected Operative Goals of the Enemy
   – Isolation, and possibly conquest of the Eastern Galilee, the Western Galilee, and the Negev.
   – Deep penetration into the Sharon and the Hefer Valley in the direction of Kalkilya–Herzliya; Tul Karem–Netanya.
   – Isolation of the three major cities (particularly Tel Aviv).
   – Cutting off the supply of vital and other services, such as water, electricity, and sewage.

B.   The British Government

The program is based upon the general assumption that, at the time of its operation, government forces will no longer be present in the country. In the event that government forces will still be present in certain bases and areas during the operation of this program, the program will need to be adjusted to this situation in those places. Special appendices will follow concerning this.

C.   International Forces

This program is based upon the assumption that no international force having effective operative power will be present in the country.

D.   Our Operative Goals

1. To defend against invasion by semi-regular and regular forces by:
   - A fixed system of defence, based upon regional defence, on the one hand; and blocking actions against the primary avenues of access of the enemy, from his territory to the territory of the state – on the other; so as to protect our settlements, essential economic enterprises, property, and the operation of government services within the territory of the state.
   - Counter-attacks, organized in advance, against enemy bases and supply lines in the depth of his territory – both within the borders of the country and in neighbouring countries.
2. To assure freedom of movement, both in the military and economic sense, within the territory of the state and in Jewish centres outside it, by conquering and holding key outposts controlling a number of transport arteries.
3. To prevent the enemy from using advance bases within his territory, which are more convenient to him for launching attacks, by conquering and holding them.
4. Economic pressure upon the enemy with the aim of forcing him to halt activities in certain parts of the country – by imposing a siege on particular cities.
5. Reducing the enemy's ability to engage in small actions by the conquest and domination of selected centres, in the countryside and in the city, within the borders of the state.
6. To seize control of government services and properties lying within the boundaries of the state, and to assure the efficient operation of necessary public services.

III.   Definition of Missions

In accordance with our operative aims, as described above, the following missions are imposed upon the various forces:

a. Strengthening the fixed defense system of the areas and adapting their activities within a district framework. In addition, blocking off the primary avenues of access of the enemy from his territory to the territory of the state, by suitable activities and arrangements.
b. Stabilizing the defense system.
c. Consolidation in large cities.
d. Control of primary national transportation arteries.
e. Siege against some of the enemy cities.

f. Conquest and dominance of the advance bases in the country.

g. Counter-attack, within and beyond the borders of the country.

IV. The Mission in Detail

A. The Fixed System of Defense

1. A fixed system of defense – within the rural areas – built upon two fundamental factors: the areas protected for circumferential defense – on the one hand; and blocking the primary avenues of access of the enemy – on the other.

2. Regional defense arrangements in the rural areas, at present primarily intended to repel a small enemy, are to be adapted in terms of planning and fortification to the projected tactical methods of a semi-regular or regular enemy, in accordance with the orders to come from the Operational Branch regarding defense and planning of rural areas.

B. Placement of Defense Systems

So as to assure effective action of the fixed defense system, as well as to assure its rear, the following actions will be performed:

1. Seizing police stations.

2. Control of government services and assuring vital services in each district.

3. Protection of secondary transport arteries.

4. Actions against enemy settlements, which are located within or adjacent to our defense system, with the goal of preventing their use as bases for active armed forces.

C. Consolidation in Large Cities

Consolidation in large cities will be performed in accordance with the following lines:

1. Seizure and domination of centres of government services and property (postal centres, telephone, railroad, police stations, ports etc.)

2. Assurance of all essential public services and enterprises.

3. Seizure and domination of all Arab neighbourhoods lying between our central urban area and the urban centre of the Arabs – particularly those neighbourhoods which dominate the avenues of entrance and exit from the cities. The dominance over these neighbourhoods will be carried out in accordance with the lines that were explained in connection with the destruction of the villages. In the event of resistance, the population will be expelled to the central, Arab urban centre.

4. Surrounding the Arab urban centre, cutting off its means of transport, and cessation of its vital services (water, electricity, gas, etc.) insofar as possible.

D. Domination over Principal National Transport Arteries

1. Seizing and controlling those objects that dominate the principal transportation arteries of the country, such as police stations, hydraulic stations, etc. These objects will be converted into fortified outposts which will serve, in accordance with need, as bases for assuring mobility (this activity will be combined, in many cases, with that of seizing police stations in order to stabilize the fixed defense system).

E.   Siege against the Enemy Cities will be conducted according to the following lines:

1. Blocking of transportation arteries leading thereto, by means of mining, blowing up bridges, and a permanent system of ambushes.
2. If necessary, by seizing the outposts which dominate traffic arteries to the enemy cities and fortifying our units over these outposts.
3. Cutting off vital services, such as: electricity, water, and gas – either by activating economic factors or by means of sabotage.
4. Action from the sea against those cities that are likely to receive supplies from the direction of the sea, with the aim of destroying the craft that bring the supplies and sabotaging the routine of the ports.

F.   Conquest and Domination of Advance Bases of the Enemy

It is not, generally speaking, the goal of this program to conquer the territory outside the borders of the Hebrew State. However, certain enemy bases which are in immediate proximity to the border and which are likely to serve as jumping points for penetration to key areas inside the state will be temporarily conquered and destroyed, in accordance with the lines sketched above, and will, until the completion of actions, be converted into part of our defense system ...

G.   Counter-Attack, within and outside the Borders of the Country

Counter-attacks will be used as an additional element in the fixed system of defense, in order to halt and to cause organised attacks to fail by semi-regular or regular enemy forces, from bases within the country or from bases beyond the borders. The counter-attacks will be carried out according to the following lines:

1. Attacks to mislead – that is, while an attack is being conducted by the enemy against a certain area of ours, a counter-attack will be waged in the depths of his own territory, in order to distract the enemy forces in the direction of the counter-attack.
2. Attacks against avenues of transport and supply, in the midst of the enemy – primarily aimed against a regular enemy which invades our borders.
3. Attacks against enemy rear bases, whether inside the country or beyond its borders.

Amir Bar-on, 'The evolution of the Army's role in strategic planning', *Israel Studies*, Vol. 1, No. 2, Fall 1996, pp. 110–14.

DOCUMENT 7   FROM THE DECLARATION OF THE
ESTABLISHMENT OF THE STATE OF ISRAEL
14 MAY 1948

Upon the expiration of the Palestine mandate, the Jewish People's Council declared the establishment of the State of Israel in the territory designated by the UN partition resolution.

... On the 29th of November 1947, the United Nations General Assembly passed a resolution calling for the establishment of a Jewish state in Eretz–

Israel; the General Assembly required the inhabitants of Eretz-Israel to take such steps as were necessary on their part for the implementation of that resolution. This recognition by the United Nations of the right of the Jewish people to establish their State is irrevocable.

This right is the natural right of the Jewish people to be masters of their own fate, like all other nations, in their own sovereign state.

Accordingly we, the members of the National Council, representing the Jewish people in Palestine and the World Zionist Movement, are assembled today, the day of termination of the British Mandate for Palestine; and by virtue of the natural and historic right of the Jewish people and of the Resolution of the General Assembly of the United Nations, we hereby proclaim the establishment of the Jewish State in Palestine to be called Medinath Yisrael (The State of Israel).

Reich, pp. 76–8.

DOCUMENT 8   FROM THE CABINET DISCUSSIONS ON THE
             CZECH ARMS DEAL   4 OCTOBER 1955

The Czech arms deal was perceived as one of the key signs that Egypt had shifted from non-alignment to a pro-Soviet position. The Cabinet discussions surrounding the arms deal reflect the globalist Cold War approach of Britain towards regional Middle Eastern tensions.

The Foreign Secretary said it was now known that the Egyptian Government had entered into a contract for the purchase of arms from the Soviet bloc. There were also indications that the Russians were making overtures for the supply of arms to Saudi Arabia, Syria and possibly other Arab countries. The implications of these developments were serious. It seemed likely that with the situation in the Far East stabilised and a situation of stalemate in Europe, the Russians were turning their attention to the Middle East. ...

The Prime Minister said that these developments might seriously affect our interests in the Middle East as a whole. Indeed, the importance of the developments in Egypt lay in their potential effect on the other Arab States. Our interests were greater than those of the United States because of our dependence on Middle East oil, and our experience in the area was greater than theirs. We should not therefore allow ourselves to be restricted over much by reluctance to act without full American concurrence and support. We should frame our policy in the light of our interests in the area and get the Americans to support it to the extent we could induce them to do so. ...

PRO CAB/128/29, CM34 (55), 4 October.

DOCUMENT 9   **THE SÈVRES PROTOCOL 24 OCTOBER 1956**

Between 22 and 24 October, British, French and Israeli representatives met at Sèvres to lay down the plans for the joint Suez–Sinai Campaign.

1 The Israeli forces launch in the evening of 29 October 1956 a large-scale attack on the Egyptian forces with the aim of reaching the Canal zone the following day.

2 On being apprised of these events, the British and French Governments during the day of 30 October 1956 respectively and simultaneously make two appeals to the Egyptian Government and the Israeli Government on the following lines:

(a) To the Egyptian Government
   (i)   halt all acts of war
   (ii) withdraw all its troops ten miles from the Canal
   (iii) accept temporary occupation of key positions on the Canal by the Anglo-French forces to guarantee freedom of passage through the Canal by vessels of all nations until a final settlement.

(b) To the Israeli Government
   (i)   halt all acts of war
   (ii) withdraw its troops ten miles to the east of the Canal.

In addition, the Israeli Government will be notified that the French and British Governments have demanded of the Egyptian Government to accept temporary occupation of key positions along the Canal by Anglo-French forces.

It is agreed that if one of the Governments refused, or did not give its consent, within twelve hours the Anglo-French forces would intervene with the means necessary to ensure that their demands are accepted.

(c) The representatives of the three Governments agree that the Israeli Government will not be required to meet the conditions in the appeal addressed to it, in the event that the Egyptian Government does not accept those in the appeal addressed to it for their part.

3 In the event that the Egyptian Government should fail to agree within the stipulated time to the conditions of the appeal addressed to it, the Anglo–French forces will launch military operations against the Egyptian forces in the early hours of the morning of 31 October.

4 The Israeli Government will send forces to occupy the western shore of the Gulf of Akaba and the group of islands Tiran and Sanafir to ensure freedom of navigation in the Gulf of Akaba.

5 Israel undertakes not to attack Jordan during the period of operations against Egypt.
But in the event that during the same period Jordan should attack Israel, the British Government undertakes not to come to the aid of Jordan.

6 The arrangements of the present protocol must remain strictly secret.

7 They will enter into force after the agreement of the three Governments.

Kyle, [75], p. 565.

DOCUMENT 10   FROM THE NATIONAL COVENANT OF THE
PALESTINE LIBERATION ORGANISATION

*On 28 May 1964, Ahmad Shukayri, chairman of the first Palestine Congress,
proclaimed the establishment of the Palestine Liberation Organisation. The
PLO's aims were outlined in a 29-article Covenant.*

Article 1. Palestine is an Arab homeland bound by strong Arab national ties
to the rest of the Arab Countries and which together form the large Arab
Homeland.

Article 2. Palestine with its boundaries at the time of the British Mandate is a
regional indivisible unit.

Article 3. The Palestinian Arab people has the legitimate right to its homeland
and is an inseparable part of the Arab Nation. It shares the sufferings and
aspirations of the Arab Nation and its struggle for freedom, sovereignty,
progress and unity.

Article 4. The people of Palestine determine its destiny when it completes the
liberation of its homeland in accordance with its own wishes and free will
and choice.

Article 6. The Palestinians are those Arab citizens who were living normally
in Palestine up to 1947, whether they remained or were expelled. Every
child who was born to a Palestinian parent after this date whether in Palestine or outside is a Palestinian.

Article 7. Jews of Palestinian origin are considered Palestinians if they are
willing to live peacefully and loyally in Palestine.

Article 10. Palestinians have three mottoes: National unity, National mobiliz-
ation, and Liberation. Once liberation is completed, the people of Palestine
shall choose for its public life whatever political, economic or social system they want.

Article 11. The Palestinian people firmly believes in Arab unity, and in order
to play its role in realizing this goal, it must, at this stage of its struggle
preserve its Palestinian personality and all its constituents. It must
strengthen the consciousness of its existence and stand against any attempt
or plan that may weaken or disintegrate its personality.

Article 12. Arab unity and the liberation of Palestine are two complementary
goals; each prepares for the attainment of the other. Arab unity leads to
the liberation of Palestine, and the liberation of Palestine leads to Arab
unity. Working for both must go side by side.

Article 13. The destiny of the Arab Nation and even the essence of Arab existence are firmly tied to the destiny of the Palestine question. From this firm
bond stems the effort and struggle of the Arab Nation to liberate Palestine.
The people of Palestine assume a vanguard role in achieving this sacred
national goal.

Article 14. The liberation of Palestine from an Arab viewpoint, is a national
duty. Its responsibilities fall upon the entire Arab Nation, governments and
peoples, the Palestinian people being in the foreground. For this purpose,

the Arab Nation must mobilize its military, spiritual and material potentialities; specifically, it must give to the Palestinian Arab people all possible support and backing and place at its disposal all opportunities and means to enable them to perform their role in liberating their homeland.

Article 16. The liberation of Palestine, from an international viewpoint, is a defensive act necessitated by the demands of self-defence as stated in the charter of the United Nations. That is why the people of Palestine, desiring to befriend all nations which love freedom, justice, and peace, look forward to their support in restoring the legitimate situation to Palestine, establishing peace and security in its territory, and enabling its people to exercise national sovereignty and freedom.

Article 17. The partitioning of Palestine in 1947 and the establishment of Israel are illegal and false regardless of the loss of time, because they were contrary to the wish of the Palestine people and its natural right to its homeland, and in violation of the basic principles embodied in the charter of the United Nations, foremost among which is the right to self-determination.

Article 18. The Balfour Declaration, the Mandate system and all that has been based upon them are considered fraud. The claims of historic and spiritual ties between Jews and Palestine are not in Agreement with the facts of history or with the true basis of sound statehood. Judaism because it is a divine religion is not a nationality with independent existence. Furthermore the Jews are not one people with an independent personality because they are citizens of the countries to which they belong.

Article 19. Zionism is a colonialist movement in its inception, aggressive and expansionist in its goals, racist and segregationist in its configuration and fascist in its means and aims. Israel in its capacity as the spearhead of this destructive movement and the pillar for colonialism is a permanent source of tension and turmoil in the Middle East in particular and to the international community in general. Because of this the people of Palestine is worthy of the support and sustenance of the community of nations.

Reich, pp. 93–6.

DOCUMENT 11   **UNSC RESOLUTION 242   22 NOVEMBER 1967**

Following the Six Day War, the United Nations Security Council adopted a British-sponsored resolution aimed at solving the Arab–Israeli conflict.

The Security Council,

Expressing its continuing concern with the grave situation in the Middle East,

Emphasizing the inadmissibility of the acquisition of territory by war and the need to work for a just and lasting peace in which every State in the area can live in security,

Emphasizing further that all Member States in their acceptance of the

Charter of the United Nations have undertaken a commitment to act in accordance with Article 2 of the Charter,

1. Affirms that the fulfilment of Charter principles requires the establishment of a just and lasting peace in the Middle East which should include the application of both the following principles:

2. 1.(i) Withdrawal of Israeli armed forces from territories occupied in the recent conflict; (ii) Termination of all claims or states of belligerency and respect for and acknowledgement of the sovereignty, territorial integrity and political independence of every State in the area and their right to live in peace within secure and recognised boundaries free from threats or acts of force; 2. Affirms further the necessity (a) For guaranteeing freedom of navigation through international waterways in the area; (b) For achieving a just settlement of the refugee problem; (c) For guaranteeing the territorial inviolability and political independence of every State in the area, through measures including the establishment of demilitarized zones; 3 Requests the Secretary-General to designate a Special Representative to proceed to the Middle East to establish and maintain contacts with the States concerned in order to promote agreement and assist efforts to achieve a peaceful and accepted settlement in accordance with the provisions and principles in this resolution; 4. Requests the Secretary-General to report to the Security Council on the progress of the efforts of the Special Representative as soon as possible.

Reich, pp. 101–2.

DOCUMENT 12   **FROM THE KHARTOUM SUMMIT**
1 SEPTEMBER 1967

Following the Six Day War, the Arab states established the framework for policy vis-à-vis Israel, the Conflict, and the territories occupied by Israel during the war.

... The Arab heads of state have agreed to unite their political efforts on the international and diplomatic level to eliminate the effects of the aggression and to ensure the withdrawal of the aggressive Israeli forces from the Arab lands which have been occupied since the 5 June aggression. This will be done within the framework of the main principle to which the Arab states adhere, namely: no peace with Israel, no recognition of Israel, no negotiations with it, and adherence to the rights of the Palestinian people in their country.

Reich, p. 101.

DOCUMENT 13   **UNSC RESOLUTION 338   22 OCTOBER 1973**

Following the 1973 October War, the United Nations Security Council adopted Resolution 338 which called for a cease-fire as well as implementation of UNSC Resolution 242.

The Security Council
1. Calls upon all parties to the present fighting to cease all firing and terminate all military activity immediately, no later than 12 hours after the moment of the adoption of this decision, in the positions they now occupy;
2. Calls upon the parties concerned to start immediately after the cease-fire the implementation of Security Council resolution 242 (1967) in all of its parts;
3. Decides that, immediately and concurrently with the cease-fire, negotiations start between the parties concerned under appropriate auspices aimed at establishing a just and durable peace in the Middle East.

Reich, p. 116.

DOCUMENT 14   **FROM SADAT'S ANNOUNCEMENT TO THE EGYPTIAN NATIONAL ASSEMBLY 9 NOVEMBER 1977**

On 9 November 1977 Egyptian President Anwar Sadat announced to the Egyptian parliament that he was willing to go to Israel to make peace. This was followed by the Israeli government's invitation and Sadat's unprecedented visit to Jerusalem on November 19th.

... I say this frankly, in your presence, to our people, to the Arab nation and to the whole world. We are ready to go to Geneva and to sit down on behalf of peace regardless of all the procedural problems raised by Israel in the hope of spoiling our chances or of exasperating us that we say, as we have done in the past, No, we do not want to go and we shall not go, so that she may appear to the world as the advocate of peace ...

... I am ready to go to Geneva – and I do not conceal this from you who are the representatives of the people and I say it in the hearing of our people and of the Arab nation. You heard me saying that I am prepared to go to the ends of this earth if my doing so will prevent any of my officers or men being killed or wounded. I really am ready to go to the ends of the earth and Israel will be amazed to hear me say that we do not refuse – I am prepared to go to their very home, to the Knesset itself and discuss things with them ...

Reich, pp. 143–4.

DOCUMENT 15   **FROM THE CAMP DAVID ACCORDS**
17 SEPTEMBER 1978

In September 1978 Egyptian President Anwar Sadat, Israeli Prime Minister Menachem Begin, and US President Jimmy Carter held a series of meetings at Camp David which resulted in the so-called Camp David Accords. These Accords provided a framework for future negotiations as well as for an Israeli–Egyptian peace treaty.

Framework for Peace in the Middle East
... To achieve a relationship of peace, in spirit of Article 2 of the United Nations Charter, future negotiations between Israel and any neighbour prepared to negotiate peace and security with it, are necessary for the purpose of carrying out all the provisions and principles of Resolutions 242 and 338.

Peace requires respect for the sovereignty, territorial integrity and political independence of every state in the area and their right to live in peace within secure and recognized boundaries free from threats or acts of force. Progress toward that goal can accelerate movement toward a new era of reconciliation in the Middle East marked by cooperation in promoting economic development, in maintaining stability, and in assuring security.

Security is enhanced by a relationship of peace and by cooperation between nations which enjoy normal relations. In addition, under the terms of peace treaties, the parties can, on the basis of reciprocity, agree to special security arrangements such as demilitarized zones, limited armament areas, early warning stations, the presence of international forces, liaisons, agreed measures for monitoring, and other arrangements that they agree are useful.

...

Taking these factors into account, the parties are determined to reach a just, comprehensive, and durable settlement of the Middle East conflict through the conclusion of peace treaties based on Security Council Resolutions 242 and 338 in all their parts. Their purpose is to achieve peace and good neighborly relations. They recognize that, for peace to endure, it must involve all those who have been most deeply affected by the conflict. They therefore agree for peace not only between Egypt and Israel, but also between Israel and each of its other neighbours which is prepared to negotiate peace with Israel on this basis. ...

Framework for the conclusion of a peace treaty between Egypt and Israel
In order to achieve peace between them, Israel and Egypt agree to negotiate in good faith with a goal of concluding within three months of the signing of this framework a peace treaty between them:

It is agreed that: The site of negotiations will be under a United Nations flag at a location or locations mutually agreed.

All of the principles of UN resolution 242 will apply in this resolution of the dispute between Israel and Egypt. Unless otherwise mutually agreed, terms of the peace treaty will be implemented between two and three years after the peace treaty is signed. The following matters are agreed between the parties:

(1)   the full exercise of Egyptian sovereignty up to the internationally recognized border between Egypt and mandated Palestine;

(2)   the withdrawal of Israeli armed forces from the Sinai;

(3)   the use of airfields left by the Israelis near Al-Arish, Rafah, Ras en-Naqb, and Sharm el-Sheikh for civilian purposes only, including possible commercial use only by all nations;

(4)   the right of free passage by ships of Israel through the Gulf of Suez and the Suez Canal on the basis of the Constantinople Convention of 1888 applying to all nations; the Strait of Tiran and Gulf of Aqaba are international waterways to be open to all nations for unimpeded and nonsuspendable freedom of navigation and overflight;

(5)   the construction of a highway between the Sinai and Jordan; and

(6)   the stationing of military forces listed below.

... After a peace treaty is signed, and after the interim withdrawal is complete, normal relations will be established between Egypt and Israel, including full recognition, including diplomatic, economic and cultural relations; termination of economic boycotts and barriers to the free movement of goods and people; and mutual protection of citizens by due process of law.

Reich, pp. 146–54.

DOCUMENT 16   **FROM THE REAGAN FRESH START**
                INITIATIVE   1 SEPTEMBER 1982

In the wake of Israel's invasion of Lebanon, the United States put forward a set of proposals to achieve a just and lasting peace known as the Fresh Start Initiative.

... The Lebanon War, tragic as it was, has left us with a new opportunity for Middle East peace. We must seize it now and bring peace to this troubled area so vital to world stability while there is still time. It was with this strong conviction that over a month ago, before the present negotiations in Beirut have been completed, I directed Secretary of State Shultz to again review our policy and to consult a wide range of outstanding Americans on the best ways to strengthen chances for peace in the Middle East. ...

But the opportunities for peace do not begin and end in Lebanon. As we help Lebanon rebuild, we must also move to resolve the root causes of conflict between Arabs and Israelis. The war in Lebanon has demonstrated many things, but two consequences are key to the peace process:

First, the military losses of the PLO have not diminished the yearning of the Palestinian people for a just solution of their claims; and

Second, while Israel's military successes in Lebanon have demonstrated that its armed forces are second to none in the region, they alone cannot bring just and lasting peace to Israel and its neighbours.

... So tonight I am calling for a fresh start. This is the moment for all those directly concerned to get involved – or lend their support – to a workable basis for peace. The Camp David agreement remains the foundation of our policy. Its language provides all parties with the leeway they need for successful negotiations.

I call on Israel to make clear that the security for which she yearns can only be achieved through genuine peace, a peace requiring magnanimity, vision, and courage.

I call on the Palestinian people to recognise that their own political aspirations are inextricably bound to recognition of Israel's right to a secure future.

And I call on the Arab states to accept the reality of Israel and the reality that peace and justice are to be gained only through hard, fair, direct negotiation. ...

Reich, pp. 175–9.

DOCUMENT 17   **FROM THE FEZ PEACE PLAN**
9 SEPTEMBER 1982

In reaction to Reagan's Fresh Start Initiative, the Arab states put forward the Fez Peace Plan at the Arab summit meeting in Fez, Morocco.

... Out of the conference's belief in the ability of the Arab nation to achieve its legitimate objectives and eliminate the aggression, and out of the principles and basis laid down by the Arab summit conferences, and out of the Arab countries' determination to continue to work by all means for the establishment of peace based on justice in the Middle East and using the plan of President Habib Bourguiba, which is based on international legitimacy, as the foundation for solving the Palestinian question and the plan of His Majesty King Fahd ibn Abd al-Aziz which deals with peace in the Middle East, and in light of the discussions and notes made by their majesties, excellencies and highnesses the kings, presidents and emirs, the conference decided to adopt the following principles:

1. The withdrawal of Israel from all Arab territories occupied in 1967 including Arab al-Kuds (Jerusalem)
2. The dismantling of settlements established by Israel on territories after 1967
3. The guarantee of freedom of worship and practice of religious rites for all religions in the holy shrines
4. The reaffirmation of the Palestinian people's right to self-determination and the exercise of its imprescriptible and inalienable national rights under the leadership of the Palestine Liberation Organisation, its sole and legitimate representative, and the indemnification of all those who do not desire to return

5. Placing the West Bank and the Gaza Strip under the control of the UN for a transitory period not exceeding a few months
6. The establishment of an independent Palestinian state with al-Kuds as its capital
7. The Security Council guarantees peace among all states of the region including the independent Palestinian state
8. The Security Council guarantees the respect of these principles.

Reich, pp. 179–80.

DOCUMENT 18   **FROM THE ISRAEL–LEBANON AGREEMENT**
17 MAY 1983

Following the 1982 Israeli invasion of Lebanon, the United States tried to broker a peace treaty between the two states. The 17 May Agreement fell short of both Israeli and Lebanese requirements and was unilaterally abrogated by Lebanon in 1984.

Article 1. 1. The Parties agree and undertake to respect the sovereignty, political independence and territorial integrity of each other. They consider the existing international boundary between Israel and Lebanon inviolable. 2. The Parties confirm that the state of war between Israel and Lebanon has been terminated and no longer exists. 3. Taking into account the provisions of paragraphs 1 and 2, Israel undertakes to withdraw all its armed forces from Lebanon in accordance with the Annex of the present Agreement.
Article 4. 1. The territory of each Party will not be used as a base for hostile or terrorist activity against the other Party, its territory, or its people. 2. Each Party will prevent the existence or organisation of irregular forces, armed bands, organisations, bases, offices or infrastructure, the aims and purposes of which include incursions or any act of terrorism into the territory of the other Party, or any other activity aimed at threatening or endangering the security of the other Party and safety of its people. To this end all agreements and arrangements enabling the presence and functioning on the territory of either Party of elements hostile to the other party are null and void. 3. Without prejudice to the inherent right of self-defence in accordance with international law, each Party will refrain: a. from organising, instigating, assisting, or participating in threats or acts of belligerency, subversion, or incitement or any aggression directed against the other Party, its population or property, both within its territory and originating therefrom, or in the territory of the other Party; b. from using the territory of a third state; c. from intervening in the internal or external affairs of the other Party. 4. Each Party undertakes to ensure that preventive action and due proceedings will be taken against persons or organisations perpetrating acts in violation of this Article.

Reich, pp. 187–91.

DOCUMENT 19   THE AMMAN AGREEMENT, OR HUSSEIN–
ARAFAT ACCORD   11 FEBRUARY 1985

On 11 February, King Hussein and Yasser Arafat signed an accord in order to create momentum for resolving the Palestine problem. The PLO's refusal to accept UN Resolutions 242 and 338 as a basis for negotiation, however, led to a breakdown in Jordanian–Palestinian relations on 19 February 1986.

The Government of the Hashemite Kingdom of Jordan and the Palestine Liberation Organisation have agreed to march together towards the realisation of a just and peaceful settlement of the Middle East problem and to put an end to the Israeli occupation of the Arab occupied territories, including Jerusalem, in accordance with the following principles:
1. Land in exchange for peace as cited in the UN resolutions, including the Security Council resolutions.
2. The Palestinian people's right to self-determination. The Palestinians will be able to exercise their inalienable right to self-determination when the Jordanians and Palestinians manage to achieve this within the framework of an Arab Confederation that it is intended to establish between the two states of Jordan and Palestine.
3. Solving the Palestinian refugee problem in accordance with the UN resolutions.
4. Solving all aspects of the Palestine question.
5. Based on this, peace negotiations should be held within the framework of an international conference to be attended by the five UN Security Council permanent member states and all parties to the conflict, including the PLO, which is the Palestinan people's sole legitimate representative, within a joint delegation – a joint Jordanian–Palestinian delegation.

Reich, pp. 194–5.

DOCUMENT 20   JORDAN RELINQUISHES ITS CLAIM TO
THE WEST BANK   31 JULY 1988

In a televised speech, King Hussein of Jordan declared that he was renouncing Jordan's claim to the West Bank which had been annexed in 1950 but had come under Israeli occupation in 1967.

... The relationship of the West Bank with the Hashemite Kingdom of Jordan in light of the PLO's call for the establishment of an independent Palestinian state, can be confined to two considerations. First, the principled consideration pertaining to the issue of Arab unity as a pan-Arab aim, to which the hearts of the Arab peoples aspire and which they want to achieve. Second, the political consideration pertaining to the extent of the Palestinian struggle's gain from the continuation of the legal relationship of the Kingdom's two banks. Our answer to the question now stems from these two considerations and the background of the clear-cut and firm Jordanian position toward the Palestine question, as we have shown.

Regarding the principle consideration, Arab unity between any two or more countries is an option of any Arab people. This is what we believe. Accordingly, we responded to the wish of the Palestinian people's representatives for unity with Jordan in 1950. From this premise, we respect the wish of the PLO, the sole and legitimate representative of the Palestinian people, to secede from us as an independent Palestinian state.

Reich, pp. 199–203.

DOCUMENT 21   **FROM THE HAMAS CHARTER**

18 AUGUST 1988

The Islamic Resistance Movement Hamas was created on 14 December 1987. Its aim is the establishment of an Islamic state in all of Palestine through Jihad.

Article 1. The Islamic Resistance Movement draws its guidelines from Islam; derives from it its thinking, interpretations and views about existence, life and humanity; refers back to it for its conduct; and is inspired by it in whatever step it takes.

Article 6. The Islamic Resistance Movement is a distinct Palestinian Movement which owes its loyalty to Allah, derives from Islam its way of life and strives to raise the banner of Allah over every inch of Palestine. Only under the shadow of Islam could the members of all regions coexist in safety and security for their lives, properties and rights. In the absence of Islam, conflict arises, oppression reigns, corruption is rampant and struggles and wars prevail...

Article 10. The Islamic Resistance Movement, while breaking its own path, will do its utmost to constitute at the same time a support to the weak, a defense to all the oppressed. It will spare no effort to implement the truth and abolish evil, in speech and in fact, both here and in any other location where it can reach out and exert influence.

Article 11. The Islamic Resistance Movement believes that the land of Palestine has been an Islamic Waqf throughout the generations and until the Day of Resurrection, no one can renounce it or part of it, or abandon it or part of it. No Arab country nor the aggregate of all Arab countries, and no Arab King or President nor all of them in the aggregate, have that right, nor has that right any organisation or the aggregate of all organisations, be they Palestinian or Arab....

Article 13. Initiatives, the so-called peaceful solutions, and the international conferences to resolve the Palestine problem, are all contrary to the beliefs of the Islamic Resistance Movement. For renouncing any part of Palestine means renouncing part of the religion; the nationalism of the Islamic Resistance Movement is part of its faith, the movement educates its members to adhere to its principles and to raise the banner of Allah over their homeland as they fight their Jihad. ...

Reich, pp. 203–12.

DOCUMENT 22   PALESTINIAN DECLARATION OF
INDEPENDENCE   15 NOVEMBER 1988

At the height of the intifada *and following Jordan's renunciation of its claim to the West Bank, PLO Chairman Yasser Arafat declared the establishment of an independent State of Palestine at the Palestine National Council in Algiers.*

In the name of God, the Compassionate, the Merciful.

Palestine, the land of the three monotheistic faiths, is where the Palestinian Arab people was born, on which it grew, developed, and excelled. The Palestinian people was never separated from or diminished in its integral bonds with Palestine. Thus the Palestinian Arab people ensured for itself an everlasting union between itself, its land, and its history. ...

When in the course of modern times a new order of values was declared with norms and values fair for all, it was the Palestinian Arab people that had been excluded from the destiny of all other peoples by a hostile array of local and foreign powers. Yet again had unaided justice been revealed as insufficient to drive the world's history along its preferred course. ...

Despite the historical injustice inflicted on the Palestinian Arab people resulting in their dispersion and depriving them of their right to self-determination, following UN General Assembly Resolution 181 (1947), which partitioned Palestine into two states, one Arab, one Jewish, yet it is this resolution that still provides these conditions of international legitimacy that ensure the right of the Palestinian Arab people to sovereignty and national independence. ...

Now by virtue of natural, historical, and legal rights and the sacrifices of successive generations who gave of themselves in defense of the freedom and independence of their homeland;

... The Palestine National Council, in the name of God, and in the name of the Palestinian Arab people, hereby proclaims the establishment of the State of Palestine on our Palestinian territory with its capital Jerusalem.

The State of Palestine is the state of Palestinians wherever they may be. The state is for them to enjoy in it their collective national and cultural identity, theirs to pursue in it a complete equality of rights. In it will be safeguarded their political and religious convictions and their human dignity by means of a parliamentary democratic system of governance, itself based on freedom of expression and the freedom to form parties. The rights of minorities will be duly respected by the majority, as minorities must abide by decisions of the majority. Governance will be based on principles of social justice, equality and nondiscrimination in public rights on grounds of race, religion, color, or sex under the aegis of a constitution which ensures the role of law and an independent judiciary. Thus all these principles shall allow no departure from Palestine's age-old spiritual and civilizational heritage of tolerance and religious co-existence. ...

Reich, pp. 213–17.

DOCUMENT 23   MADRID CONFERENCE LETTER OF
INVITATION   18 OCTOBER 1991

The 1990/91 Gulf War opened a window of opportunity for resolving conflict in the Middle East. Israel, Jordan, Lebanon, Syria and the Palestinians were invited to an international peace conference in Madrid, which set up the framework for further negotiations.

After extensive consultations with Arab states, Israel and the Palestinians, the United States and the Soviet Union believe that an historic opportunity exists to advance the prospects for genuine peace throughout the region. The United States and the Soviet Union are prepared to assist the parties to achieve a just, lasting and comprehensive peace settlement, through direct negotiations along two tracks, between Israel and the Arab states, and between Israel and the Palestinians, based on United Nations Security Council Resolutions 242 and 338. The objective of this process is real peace.

Toward that end, the president of the US and the president of the USSR invite you to a peace conference, which their countries will co-sponsor, followed immediately by direct negotiations. The conference will be convened in Madrid on October 30, 1991.

... Direct bilateral negotiations will begin four days after the opening of the conference. Those parties who wish to attend multilateral negotiations will convene two weeks after the opening of the conference to organise those negotiations. The co-sponsors believe that those negotiations should focus on region-wide issues of water, refugee issues, environment, economic development, and other subjects of mutual interest.

The co-sponsors will chair the conference, which will be held at ministerial level. Governments to be invited include Israel, Syria, Lebanon and Jordan. Palestinians will be invited and attend as part of a joint Jordanian–Palestinian delegation. Egypt will be invited to the conference as a participant. The European Community will be a participant in the conference, alongside the United States and the Soviet Union and will be represented by its presidency. The

Gulf Cooperation Council will be invited to send its secretary-general to the conference as an observer, and GCC member states will be invited to participate in organising the negotiations on multilateral issues. The United Nations will be invited to send an observer, representing the secretary-general.

The conference will have no power to impose solutions on the parties or veto agreements reached by them. It will have no authority to make decisions for the parties and no ability to vote on issues of results. The conference can reconvene only with the consent of all parties. ...

Reich, pp. 226–8.

DOCUMENT 24   **FROM THE DECLARATION OF PRINCIPLES 9 SEPTEMBER 1993**

Months of secret negotiations in Norway culminated in the signing of the first Israeli–Palestinian Agreement known as the Declaration of Principles, or Oslo (I) Accords.

The Government of the State of Israel and PLO team ... representing the Palestinian people, agree that it is time to put an end to decades of confrontation and conflict, recognize their mutual legitimate and political rights, and strive to live in peaceful coexistence and mutual dignity and security and achieve a just, lasting and comprehensive peace settlement and historic reconciliation through the agreed political process. Accordingly, the two sides agree to the following principles:

Article 1.

The aim of the Israeli–Palestinian negotiations within the current Middle East peace process is, among other things, to establish a Palestinian Interim Self–Government Authority, the elected Council for the Palestinian people in the West Bank and the Gaza Strip, for a transitional period not exceeding five years, leading to permanent settlement based on Security Council Resolutions 242 and 338.

It is understood that the interim arrangements are an integral part of the whole peace process and that the negotiations on the permanent status will lead to the implementation of Security Council Resolution 242 and 338.

Article 2.

The agreed framework for the interim period is set forth in this Declaration of Principles.

Article 3. Elections

1. In order that the Palestinian people in the West Bank and Gaza Strip may govern themselves according to democratic principles, direct, free and general political elections will be held for the Council under agreed supervision and international observation, while the Palestinian police will ensure public order.

2. An agreement will be concluded on the exact mode and conditions of the elections in accordance with the protocol attached to Annex I, with the goal of holding the elections not later than nine months after the entry into force of this Declaration of Principles.

3. These elections will constitute a significant interim preparatory step toward the realisation of the legitimate rights of the Palestinian people and their just requirements.

Article 4. Jurisdiction

Jurisdiction of the Council will cover West Bank and Gaza territory, except for issues that will be negotiated in the permanent status negotiations. The two sides view the West Bank and Gaza Strip as a single territorial unit, whose integrity will be preserved during the interim period.

Article 5. Transitional Period and Permanent Status Negotiations

1. The five-year transitional period will begin upon the withdrawal from the Gaza Strip and Jericho area.

2. Permanent status negotiations will commence as soon as possible, but not later than the beginning of the third year of the interim period, between the Government of Israel and the Palestinian people representatives.

3. It is understood that these negotiations shall cover remaining issues, including: Jerusalem, refugees, settlements, security arrangements, borders, relations and cooperation with other neighbours, and other issues of common interest.

4. The two parties agree that the outcome of the permanent status negotiations should not be prejudiced or preempted by agreements reached for the interim period.

Reich, pp. 230–4.

DOCUMENT 25   **JORDANIAN–ISRAEL PEACE AGREEMENT**
26 OCTOBER 1994

On 26 October 1994, Jordanian Prime Minister Abdul–Salam Majali and Israeli Prime Minister Itzhak Rabin met in the Jordan Valley to sign the Israeli–Jordanian Peace Agreement.

Article 1. Establishment of Peace.

Peace is hereby established between the State of Israel and the Hashemite Kingdom of Jordan (the Parties) effective from the exchange of the instruments of ratification of this Treaty.

Article 2. General Principles.

The Parties will apply between them the provisions of the Charter of the United Nations and the principles of international law governing relations among states in times of peace. In particular: 1. They recognise and will respect each other's sovereignty, territorial integrity and political independence; 2. They recognise and will respect each other's right to live in peace within secure and recognised boundaries; 3. They will develop good neighbourly relations of co-operation between them to ensure lasting security, will refrain from the threat or use of force against each other and will settle all disputes between them by peaceful means; ...

Article 4. Security.

1.a. Both Parties, acknowledging that mutual understanding and co-operation in security-related matters will form a significant part of their relations and will further enhance the security of the region, take upon themselves to base their security relations on mutual trust, advancement of joint interests and co-operation, and to aim towards a regional framework of partnership in peace. ... 2. The obligations referred to in this Article are without prejudice to the inherent right of self-defence in accordance with the United Nations Charter. 3. The Parties undertake, in accordance with the provisions of this Article, the following: a. to refrain from the threat or use of force or weapons, conventional, non-conventional or of any other kind, against each other, or of other actions or activities that adversely affect the security of the other Party; b. to refrain from organising, instigating, inciting, assisting or participating in acts or threats of belligerency, hostility, subversion or violence against the other Party; c. to take necessary and effective measures to ensure that acts or threats of belligerency, hostility, subversion or violence against the other Party do not originate from, are not committed within, through or over their territory. ...

Article 7. Economic Relations.

1.Viewing economic development and prosperity as pillars of peace, security and harmonious relations between states, peoples and individual human beings, the Parties, taking note of understandings reached between them, affirm their mutual desire to promote economic co-operation between them, as well as within the framework of wider regional economic co-operation. 2. In order to accomplish this goal, the Parties agree to the following: a. to remove all discriminatory barriers to normal economic relations, to terminate economic boycotts directed at each other, and to co-operate in terminating boycotts directed against either Party by third parties; b. recognising that the principle of free and unimpeded flow of goods and services should guide their relations, the Parties will enter into negotiations with a view to concluding agreements on economic co-operation, including trade and the establishment of a free trade area, investment, banking, industrial co-operation and labour, for the purpose of promoting beneficial economic relations ...

Reich, pp. 263–73.

CHRONOLOGY OF EVENTS

	11 August, King Talal is succeeded by King Hussein
1953	14 October, Qibya raid
1955	28 February, Gaza raid
1956	26 July, Nasser nationalises the Suez Canal
	29 October, Israel invades Sinai
	5 November, Britain and France invade Suez Canal zone
	6–7 November, Britain, France and Israel agree to cease-fire
1957	5 January, Eisenhower Doctrine
1958	February, UAR created
	14 July, Iraqi monarchy is overthrown
1964	January, PLO is created
	May, First PNC in Jerusalem
1966	November, Syrian–Egyptian defence pact
	13 November, As-Samu raid
1967	April, Israeli–Syrian air clash
	13 May, Soviet Union tells Egypt of pending Israeli attack on Syria
	17 May, Nasser mobilises troops
	18 May, UNEF asked to withdraw
	23 May, Blockade of Straits of Tiran
	30 May, Egyptian–Jordanian defence pact
	5–10 June, Six Day War
	September, Khartoum summit
	22 November, UN Resolution 242
1968	21 March, Battle of Karameh
	October, Hafez al-Asad assumes leadership of Syria
	December, Beirut raid
1969	February, Yasser Arafat is elected PLO chairman
	War of Attrition begins
	9 December, Rogers Plan
1970	25 June, War of Attrition ends
	September, Black September*
	28 September, Nasser dies; Anwar Sadat assumes the presidency
1971	27 May, Soviet–Egyptian Treaty of Friendship
	28 November, Wasfi al-Tell is assassinated
1972	March, King Hussein's Confederation Plan
	July, Sadat expels Soviet advisors
1973	6–22 October, October War
	22 October, UN Resolution 338
	11 November, Israeli–Egyptian cease-fire
	21 December, Geneva Peace Conference
1974	1 January, Israeli–Egyptian disengagement agreement
	31 May, Israeli–Syrian disengagement agreement
	October, PLO becomes sole legitimate representative of the Palestinian people
	13 November, PLO granted UN observer status

1975	April, Lebanese civil war begins
	1 September, Sinai II Agreement
1977	9 November, Sadat is prepared to go to Jerusalem
	19–20 November, Sadat addresses Knesset
	25–26 December, Begin meets Sadat in Ismailia
1978	14 March, Operation Litani
	5–17 September, Camp David Summit
1979	26 March, Israeli–Egyptian Peace Treaty is signed
	31 March, Arab League expels Egypt
1981	7 June, Israel bombs Iraqi nuclear reactor
	6 October, Sadat is assassinated
	14 December, Israel annexes Golan Heights
1982	6 June, Israel invades Lebanon
	August, Multinational peacekeeping force enters Beirut
	14 September, Bashir Gemayel is assassinated
	17–18 September, Sabra and Shatilla massacres
	9 October, PLO–Jordanian negotiations start
1983	10 April, PLO–Jordanian negotiations break down
	17 May, Israeli–Lebanese Agreement
	16 September, Israel begins withdrawal from Lebanon
1984	21 February, US forces leave Lebanon
	5 March, Lebanon abrogates agreement with Israel
1985	11 February, Jordanian–PLO negotiations
	July, Israel completes withdrawal to security zone
1986	March, King Hussein breaks relations with Arafat
1987	April, Arafat abrogates agreement with Jordan
	9 December, Intifada erupts; Hamas is created
1988	16 April, Khalil al-Wazir is assassinated in Tunis
	31 July, Jordan severs ties to the West Bank
	15 November, Palestinian state is declared
	14 December, PLO renounces terrorism
	US–PLO dialogue begins
1989	6 April, Israel announces election plan for the Occupied Territories
	22 May, Egypt is re-admitted to the Arab League
	September, Mubarak announces 10-point plan
1990	20 June, US suspends dialogue with PLO
	2 August, Iraq invades Kuwait
	12 October, Arafat supports Saddam Hussein
1991	16 January, Operation Desert Storm is launched
	Scud missiles are launched against Israel and Saudi Arabia
	27 February, Bush announces liberation of Kuwait
	March, Baker's shuttle diplomacy begins
	30 October, Madrid Peace Conference is convened
1992	July, Yitzhak Rabin forms new Israeli government
1993	Spring, Secret PLO–Israel negotiations in Oslo
	July, Operation Accountability

13 September, Israel–PLO Declaration of Principles

1 October, Washington conference on the Middle East

1994 25 February, Jewish settler kills Palestinian worshippers in Hebron

Israel–PLO talks suspended

31 March, Israel–PLO talks resume

29 April, Israel–PLO agreement on framework for economic ties

4 May, Gaza–Jericho Agreement

18 May, Israel completes withdrawal of troops from Gaza

25 July, Summit meeting in Washington between Rabin and King Hussein

Washington Declaration

29 September, Oslo Declaration

1 October, Secondary and tertiary boycotts of Israel are lifted

9 October, Hamas gunmen kill 2 and wound 13 in Jerusalem

19 October, Hamas suicide bomber kills 22 and wounds 26 on Tel Aviv bus

26 October, Jordanian–Israeli Peace Treaty

18 November, Palestinian police fire on demonstrators in Gaza, killing 12

10 December, Rabin and Arafat receive Nobel Peace Prize

1995 22 January, Islamic Jihad kill 19 and wound 62 in an attack on Beit Lid junction

4 November, Assassination of Israeli Prime Minister Yitzhak Rabin

5 December, Yigal Amir is charged with premeditated murder of Rabin

10 December, Israeli troops redeploy from Palestinian city of Tulkarem

21 December, Talks between PNA and Hamas end unsuccessfully

27 December, Israeli troops withdraw from Ramallah

1996 5 January, Israeli security services kill Hamas activist Yahya Ayash by booby-trapping his mobile phone

20 January, Palestinian elections; Arafat is elected president of the PNA

25 February, Hamas suicide bombs on Jerusalem bus and in the city of Ashkelon, killing 25, injuring 77

4 March, Suicide bomb explodes outside Tel Aviv shopping centre, killing 12, wounding 126

7 March, Newly-elected PNC is inaugurated in Gaza City

27 March, Yigal Amir is convicted of murdering Rabin

11–26 April, Operation Grapes of Wrath

5 May, Israeli–Palestinian final status negotiations scheduled for completion by May 1999

29 May, Israeli elections; Benjamin Netanyahu becomes Prime Minister by 50.4% to 49.6%

June 16, Netanyahu issues policy guidelines stating opposition to a

Palestinian state, the strengthening of settlements, the retention of Jerusalem and the Golan Heights

23–28 September, Temple Mount riots

2 October, Two-day White House Mideast summit ends without results

1997   9 January, Two pipe bombs explode in Tel Aviv, wounding 13

15 January, Netanyahu and Arafat agree to the withdrawal of 80% of Israeli troops from Hebron and other areas of the West Bank by mid-1998

17 January, Hebron reverts to Palestinian control

4 February, Two Israeli helicopters transporting troops to South Lebanon collide, killing 73

13 February, Clinton urges resumption of Israeli–Syrian talks

17 February, Netanyahu vows to strengthen his hold over Jerusalem

26 February, Knesset approves of construction of Har Homa settlement

5 March, Arafat tells Jewish leaders in New York that Palestinian Covenant has been changed so that it no longer calls for the destruction of Israel

13 March, Jordanian border-guard fires on Israeli schoolgirls, killing 7 and wounding 6 more

27 March, Suicide bomber kills 3 in Tel Aviv café

31 March, Arab League freezes relations with Israel and reinstates economic boycott

30 July, Two suicide bombs explode in Jerusalem market Mahane Yehuda killing 13 and wounding 150

4 September, Three suicide bombers explode bombs in Jerusalem's Ben Yehuda Street, killing 4 and wounding 180

5 September, Netanyahu announces that he no longer considers Oslo Accords binding

26 September, Mossad agents try unsuccessfully to assassinate Hamas political leader Khaled Meshal in Jordan

1 October, Israel releases Hamas founder Sheikh Ahmad Yassin (imprisoned since 1989)

13 November, Arafat states that he will declare statehood in 1999 regardless of the status of negotiations with Israel

CAST OF CHARACTERS

Abdallah (1882–1951): Second son of the Sharif of Mecca; Amir of Transjordan 1921–46; King of Transjordan 1946–48; King of Jordan 1948–51. Regarded as a collaborator with the British and the Jews, he was assassinated on 20 July 1951 by a Palestinian, while entering the al-Aqsa Mosque in Jerusalem.

Abu Jihad: Palestinian guerrilla. Second in command to Arafat; assassinated in Tunis.

Ali, Ahmad Ismail: Egyptian Defence Minister during the 1973 October War.

Arafat, Yasser (b.1929): Palestinian guerrilla leader and politician since 1958; founding member of Fatah; became Chairman of the PLO Executive in1969; was appointed Commander-in-Chief of Palestinian Arab guerrilla forces in 1970; signed the Oslo Accords with Israel in 1993; elected Palestinian President in 1996.

Al-Asad, Hafez: Syrian officer and politician of Alawi origin; appointed Commander of the Syrian Air Force in 1963; led *coup d'état* in 1966; Syrian Prime Minister 1970–71; Syrian President since 1971.

Ashrawi, Hanan Michail (b.1946): Palestinian politician; member of the Palestinian delegation to the Madrid peace conference; elected to the Palestinian Authority in 1996.

Begin, Menachem (1913–92): Zionist underground leader and Israeli politician. Head of the militant underground organisation Irgun 1943–48; founder of the Herut Party in 1948; Minister without portfolio in the 1967 National Unity Government; resigned post in 1970; elected first Likud Prime Minister in 1977; withdrew from politics after the Sabra and Shatilla massacres in Lebanon in 1982; resigned from office in 1983.

Ben Gurion, David (1886–1973): Israeli politician. First Secretary-General of the Histadrut in 1920; elected chairman of the Zionist Executive and

Jewish Agency in 1935; became first Israeli Prime Minister and Defence Minister in 1948; left the government in 1953; returned first as Defence Minister and then Prime Minister in 1955; resigned in 1963.

Bernadotte, Count Folke (1895–1948):   A Swedish nobleman and President of the Swedish Red Cross; appointed UN mediator for Palestine in May 1948; recommended merger of Arab Palestine with Jordan; suggested that Haifa be made international port and Lydda international airport; he was assassinated on 17 September 1948 by Jewish extremists.

Breznev, Leonid (1906–82):   Soviet officer and politician. Elected deputy to Supreme Soviet of USSR in 1950; elected to Central Committee of the Communist Party in 1952; President of the Supreme Soviet 1960–63; elected First Secretary of the Central Committee of the Communist Party of the Soviet Union in 1964; title changed to General Secretary in 1966.

Carter, Jimmy (b.1924):   US politician. Entered state politics in 1962 after seven years' service as a naval officer; US President 1977–81.

Dayan, Moshe (1915–81):   Israeli military and political leader; lost his eye in 1941 in an Allied operation against Vichy France in Lebanon; led the IDF to victory in the Sinai campaign; left army in 1957 to enter politics; Minister of Agriculture 1959–64; Minister of Defence in June 1967.

Dulles, John Foster (1888–1959):   US Secretary of State under Eisenhower; Cold War hardliner; wanted to create a Middle East defence organisation; played a decisive role in US Middle East policy during the Suez Crisis.

Eisenhower, Dwight (1890–1969):   US general and politician. Commanding General of US forces in Europe during the Second World War; assumed supreme command over NATO forces in 1951; US president 1953–61.

Eshkol, Levi (1895–1969):   Zionist Labour leader and Israeli politician. Minister of Agriculture 1951–52; Minister of Finance 1952–63; Prime Minister 1963–69; Defence Minister 1963–67.

Farouk, King of Egypt (1920–65):   Son of King Fu'ad; educated in England and Egypt; inherited the throne in 1936; deposed in July 1952 by the Free Officers; went into exile to Italy.

Ford, Gerald (b.1913):   US politician. Elected to Congress in 1948; became Vice-President under Nixon; became US President in 1974 upon Nixon's resignation; US President 1974–77.

Gemayel, Bashir (1947–82):   Lebanese politician and militia leader. Appointed political director of Kataib Party (Ashrafieh district) in 1972;

became Commander-in-Chief of the Kataib Military Council in 1976; appointed head of unified command of Lebanese Forces in 1976; became Commander-in Chief of Lebanese Forces in 1980; elected Lebanese President in 1982; was killed before he could assume office in September 1982.

Haig, Alexander (b.1924): US officer and politician. Supreme Allied Commander in Europe 1974–79; Secretary of State under Reagan 1981–82.

Herzl, Theodor (1860–1904): Father of political Zionism; founder of World Zionist Organisation; author of *Der Judenstaat* (The Jewish State); organised the first Zionist Congress in Basle in 1897.

Hussein, King of Jordan (b.1935): Born in Amman; educated in Egypt and England; crowned in 1953; signed defence treaty with Egypt in May 1967; expelled PLO from Jordan in 1970; signed peace with Israel in 1994.

Al-Husseini, Hajj Amin (1894–1974): Palestinan political and religious leader; headed anti-Jewish demonstrations in 1920; became Mufti of Jerusalem in 1921; elected president of the Supreme Muslim Council in 1922; elected president of Arab Higher Committee in 1936; led Arab revolt 1936–37; escaped to Syria and then to Germany where he worked for the Nazis as a propagandist; tried to form an 'All Palestine Government' in Gaza in 1948; moved to Lebanon.

Khalaf, Salah (1933–91): Palestinian guerrilla. Fatah leader upon the establishment of the resistance movement in 1957.

Kissinger, Henry (b. 1923): US politician. Served in the Army 1943–46; member of faculty of Harvard University 1954–69; received Nobel Peace Prize in 1973; US Secretary of State 1973–77; Assistant to President for National Security Affairs until 1975.

McMahon, Henry (1862–1949): British High Commissioner in Egypt 1914–16; accepted principles of Arab independence in correspondence with the Sharif Hussein of Mecca.

Meir, Golda (1898–1978): Zionist leader and Israeli politician. Active in the Histadrut; member of the Political Department of the Jewish Agency in 1936; met secretly with King Abdallah of Jordan in an effort to reach an agreement in 1947; member of Knesset since 1949; Minister of Labour 1949–56; Foreign Minister 1956–66; appointed Secretary-General of Mapai in 1965; Prime Minister 1969–73.

Mubarak, Hosni (b.1949): Egyptian officer and politician. Vice-President under Sadat; became President upon Sadat's assassination in 1981.

Muhieddin, Zakariya (b.1918):   Egyptian officer and politician. Joined Free Officer coup in 1952; Minister of Interior 1953–56; Prime Minister 1965–66; Vice-President 1966–67; removed from government 1968.

Nasser, Gamal Abdel (1918–70):   Egyptian officer and politician. Participant in 1952 Free Officers Coup; Deputy Secretary of the Revolutionary Council in 1953; Prime Minister in 1954; elected President in 1956; promoted doctrine of Arab Socialism.

Netanyahu, Benjamin (b. 1949):   Israeli politician. Israeli Ambassador to UN 1984–88; elected Likud Member of Knesset in 1988; elected Israeli Prime Minister in 1996.

Peres, Shimon (b. 1923):   Israeli statesman. Deputy Director of the Ministry of Defence in 1952; Director General of the Ministry of Defence 1953–65; Defence Minister 1974–77; acting Prime Minister after Yitzhak Rabin's assassination November 1995 – May 1996.

Pyrlin, Evgeny: Head of the Egypt Department, Soviet Foreign Ministry, during the 1967 June War.

Rabin, Yitzhak (1922–95):   Israeli general and politician. Chief of Staff in 1964; Israeli Prime Minister 1974–77; Defence Minister in 1984; Prime Minister 1992–95; signed Oslo Accords with PLO.

Sadat, Anwar (1918–81):   Egyptian officer and politician. One of the leaders of the Free Officers; participated in 1952 coup; Chairman of the National Assembly, 1959–69; appointed Vice-President in 1969; succeeded Nasser as President after Nasser's death in 1970; signed peace with Israel in 1979; assassinated by Islamists in 1981.

Samuel, Sir Herbert (1870–1963):   British liberal statesman. Helped prepare the ground for the Balfour Declaration; first High Commissioner of Palestine 1920–25; drafted 1922 White Paper; after Second World War opposed partition of Palestine.

Sharett, Moshe (1894–1965):   Zionist Labour leader and Israeli politician. Appointed head of Political Department of Jewish Agency in 1933; chief Zionist spokesman to the British and the Arabs; Israeli Foreign Minister 1948–56; Chairman of the Zionist and Jewish Agency Executive 1960–65.

Sharon, Ariel (b. 1928):   Israeli general and politician. Elected Likud Member of Knesset in 1974; Special Adviser to Rabin 1975–76; Minister of Agriculture 1977–81; Minister of Defence 1981–82; Minister without portfolio 1982–84.

Al-Shukayri, Ahmad (b.1907): Palestinian politician; headed Palestinian propaganda office in the US in 1946; member of Syrian delegation to the UN 1949–50; Under-Secretary for Political Affairs of the Arab League 1951–57; Saudi Arabian Minister of State for UN Affairs and Ambassador to UN 1957–62; Palestinian Representative to Arab League in 1963; Chairman of PLO 1964–69.

Vance, Cyrus (b.1917): US politician. Secretary of State under Carter 1977–80; resigned over Carter's decision to attempt a rescue of the hostages in Iran.

Wazir, Khalil: Palestinian guerrilla. Fatah leader upon the establishment of the resistance movement in 1957.

Weizmann, Chaim (1874–1952): Chemistry professor and Zionist leader; president of Zionist Organisation 1920–48; supported partition on the grounds of parity in Palestine; first President of Israel 1948–52.

GLOSSARY

Aliyah (Hebrew: ascent)   Wave of Jewish immigration to Palestine and, later, to Israel.

Arab Higher Committee   The main institution of the Palestinian–Arab political leadership in 1936 under the chairmanship of Hajj Amin al-Husseini. Outlawed on 1 October 1937 for its role in the 1936 Arab Revolt.

Arab League   Established in 1945 by Egypt, Iraq, Lebanon, Saudi Arabia, Syria, Transjordan and Yemen to promote Arab co-operation and co-ordination as well as providing a united political front.

Arab Legion   Army formed in Transjordan in 1920–21 by the British. Precursor of the Jordanian Army.

Arab Liberation Army   Arab force during the 1947–48 Arab–Israeli war.

Ashkenazim   Jews of east European origin.

Bar Lev Line   Unofficial name for the system of Israeli fortresses along the Suez Canal during the time of the War of Attrition, 1968–69.

Black September   Confrontation between the Jordanian Army and Palestinian guerrillas in Jordan in September 1970, as a result of which the PLO was expelled from Jordan and relocated its headquarters to Beirut, Lebanon.

Circassians   Originally from the area of the Caucasus, many emigrated to the Ottoman Empire when the Russians took control. The Muslim Circassians settled in Syria, Jordan, and Palestine where they assimilated with the local population.

Dalet   Hebrew letter of the alphabet, corresponding to D.

DFLP   Democratic Front for the Liberation of Palestine.

Diaspora   Term for 'dispersion' of the Jews.

DOP   Declaration of Principles; also known as the Oslo Acccord.

Druze   Originally an offshoot of Ismaili Shi'ism, but considered by most to have seceded from Islam. Their spiritual guide was the Fatimid Caliph Hakim in the 11th century. The Druze stress moral and social principles rather than ritual and ceremony. Most settled in Lebanon, Syria and Palestine.

Eretz Yisrael (Hebrew: Land of Israel)   Hebrew name of Palestine in its original mandate boundaries (including Jordan).

Fatah   Palestinian guerrilla organisation founded in 1957 in Kuwait by, amongst others, Yasser Arafat. Became the core of the PLO.

Fedayeen (Arabic: suicide squads, commandos)   Generally means Palestinian guerrillas.

Green Line   Armistice frontiers in 1949; pre-1967 Six Day War Israeli state boundary.

Gush Emunim (Hebrew: Bloc of Believers)   Religious Zionist movement established in the wake of the Six Day War, whose aims include, among others, to integrate the territories gained in that war into the Israeli state on the grounds that they are part of the Land of Israel.

Haganah (Hebrew: defence)   Jewish underground organisation established in 1920 following the Arab riots and British failure to defend the Jews. It became the core of the Israel Defence Force upon the declaration of the State of Israel in 1948.

Hamas (Arabic acronym for Islamist Resistance Movement)   Founded in 1987 in the Gaza Strip; opposes peace with Israel.

Hashemites   Clan of the Qureish tribe from whom the Prophet Mohammed is descended. Has come to refer to the Sharifs of Mecca, who supplied the kings for the Hejaz, Iraq, and Jordan.

Herut   Israeli party established in 1948 by veterans of the Irgun; headed by Menachem Begin; advocated an activist approach to the Arab states as well as assertion of Jewish rights on both sides of the Jordan river.

Histadrut   General Labour Federation in Israel. Established in 1920 for Jewish workers; opened its doors to Arab workers in 1969.

Hizbollah (Arabic: Party of God) Lebanese Shi'a resistance movement established in the wake of the 1982 Israeli invasion of Lebanon.

IDF Israel Defence Force.

Intifada (Arabic: shaking off) Name given to the Palestinian uprising against Israeli occupation which began on 9 December 1987 and lasted until the signing of the 1993 Oslo Accords between the PLO and Israel.

Irgun Zvai Leumi (Hebrew: National Military Organisation) Jewish extremist underground organisation founded in 1937. After the 1939 White Paper the Irgun directed its operations against the British. In 1946 the Irgun blew up the British Army Command and the Palestine Government Secretariat in the King David Hotel.

Jewish Agency Formally established in 1929 to facilitate Jewish immigration to Palestine, to advance the Hebrew language and culture, to purchase land in Palestine, to develop Jewish agriculture and settlements, and to fulfil Jewish religious needs in Palestine. The Jewish Agency also functioned as a quasi government internationally until those functions were taken over by the Israeli government in 1948.

Kach Militant nationalist and religious Zionist Israeli party.

Kataib (Arabic: phalanx) Paramilitary youth movement in Lebanon established in 1936 by Pierre Gemayel, George Naccache, Charles Helou and Shafiq Wasif to work for Lebanese indepedence. Evolved into a Maronite Christian organisation with a party and militia devoted to preserving the Christian character of Lebanon.

Kibbutz Collective agricultural settlement in Israel, based upon equal sharing in both production and consumption; product of the difficult living conditions in Palestine at the beginning of the century as well as the socialism adhered to by the Zionist leaders at that time.

Land of Israel Movement Established in the aftermath of the 1967 Six Day War in opposition to Israeli withdrawal from the occupied territories.

An-Nakba (Arabic: the disaster) Term for the Palestinian experience in the 1948 war, alluding to the Arab defeat and the Palestinian refugee situation.

National Religious Party Established in 1955 when the two religious Zionist parties Mizrahi and Hapoel HaMizrahi merged; aimed at restoring religious values and the Torah as Israel's constitution; believes in Jewish historical rights to the whole of Palestine; is in favour of settlement of the West Bank.

NATO   North Atlantic Treaty Organisation.

OPEC   Organisation of Petroleum Exporting Countries.

PCP   Palestine Communist Party.

PFLP   Popular Front for the Liberation of Palestine.

PLA   Palestine Liberation Army.

PLO   Palestine Liberation Organisation.

PNA   Palestine National Authority

PNC   Palestine National Council.

PNM   Palestinian National Movement.

Sephardim   Eastern or Oriental Jews.

SLA   South Lebanese Army.

Sumud (Arabic: steadfastness)   Term used to describe the Palestinian pursuit of unity and endurance of hardship during the Intifada.

Takfir wa al-Hijra (Arabic: penitence and withdrawal)   Egyptian Islamist group established in 1973; called for a return to a state of 'pure' Islam; kidnapped and murdered an ex-government minister in 1977; responsible for bombings and killings in Cairo as well as attempts to overthrow the Egyptian government; responsible for the assassination of Egyptian President Anwar Sadat in 1981.

Tehiya (Hebrew: renaissance)   Militant nationalist Israeli party; broke away from the Likud Party in 1978 in opposition to the Camp David peace agreement.

Territorial maximalism   Agenda pursued by religious Zionists and right-wing Israelis to integrate the territories occupied after 1967 into Israel on either religious or security grounds. Sees Israel's boundary as the Jordan river.

Transjordan   The area east of the Jordan river; included in the British mandate; in 1921 the British established Transjordan; in 1948 the name was changed to the Hashemite Kingdom of Jordan.

UNC   Unified National Command.

UNEF   United Nations Emergency Force.

UNSC   United Nations Security Council.

UNSCOP   United Nations Special Committee on Palestine.

Wafd   Egyptian nationalist party; evolved from the Egyptian delegation sent to negotiate Egyptian independence from the British in 1919; was in power in 1924, 1928, 1930, 1936–37, 1942–44, 1950 and 1952.

Wailing Wall   Built by King Herod in 20 BC as the western wall of the Temple in Jerusalem; only remnant of the Temple after its destruction by the Romans in AD 70; most hallowed site in Judaism.

Waqf   Muslim religious foundation or endowment.

Yishuv   (Hebrew: settlement) The Jewish settlement in Palestine before the establishment of the State of Israel.

Yom Kippur   (Hebrew: Day of Atonement)   After the Sabbath, the most important of the Jewish holy days; marked by 24 hours of fasting and prayer.

Zero sum   Belief that the gain of one party to a conflict automatically translates into the loss of the other party, thus making compromise difficult.

BIBLIOGRAPHY

The place of publication is London unless otherwise stated.

1   Abbas, Mahmoud, *Through Secret Channels*, Garnet Publishing, Reading, 1995.
2   Abu Amr, Ziad, *Islamic Fundamentalism in the West Bank and Gaza*, Indiana University Press, Bloomington, 1994.
3   Abu Lughod, Ibrahim, *The Arab–Israeli Confrontation of June 1967: An Arab Perspective*, Northwest University Press, Evanston, 1987.
4   Adan, Avraham, *The Yom Kippur War: An Israeli General's Account*, Drum Books, New York, 1986.
5   Ajami, Fuad, *The Arab Predicament: Arab Political Thought and Practice since 1967*, Cambridge University Press, Cambridge, 1981.
6   Alteras, Isaac, *Eisenhower and Israel: US–Israeli Relations, 1953–1960*, University Press of Florida, Gainesville, 1993.
7   Amos, John W., *Palestinian Resistance: Organisation of a National Movement*, Pergamon, New York, 1980.
8   Antonius, George, *The Arab Awakening: The Story of the Arab National Movement*, Capricorn Books, New York, 1965.
9   Ashrawi, Hanan, *This Side of Peace: A Personal Account*, Simon & Schuster, New York, 1995.
10 Avineri, Shlomo, *The Making of Modern Zionism: The Intellectual Origins of the Jewish State*, Basic Books, New York, 1981.
11 Bailey, Sidney D., *Four Arab–Israeli Wars and the Peace Process*, Macmillan, 1990.
12 Ball, George, *Error and Betrayal in Lebanon: An Analysis of Israel's Invasion of Lebanon and the Implications for US–Israeli Relations*, Foundation for Middle East Peace, Washington DC, 1984.
13 Baram, Amatzia, 'The Iraqi invasion of Kuwait: decision-making in Baghdad' in Amatzia Baram and Barry Rubin, *Iraq's Road to War*, St Martin's Press, New York, 1993.
14 Bar On, Mordechai, *The Gates of Gaza: Israel's Road to Suez and Back, 1955–1957*, St Martin's Griffin, New York, 1994.
15 Bar Siman Tov, Yaacov, *The War of Attrition*, Columbia University Press, New York, 1980.

16   Bar Siman Tov, Yaacov, *Israel and the Peace Process, 1977–1982: In Search of Legitimacy for Peace*, State University of New York Press, Albany, 1994.

17   Bar Zohar, Michael, *Ben Gurion: A Biography*, Weidenfeld & Nicolson, New York, 1978.

18   Becker, Jillian, *The PLO: Rise and Fall of the Palestine Liberation Organisation*, St Martin's Press, New York, 1984.

19   Benziman, Uzi, *Sharon: An Israeli Caesar*, Robson Books, 1987.

20   Black, Ian and Morris, Benny, *Israel's Secret Wars: The Untold History of Israeli Intelligence*, Hamish Hamilton, 1991.

21   Brand, Laurie A., *Palestinians in the Arab World: Institution Building and the Search for State*, Columbia University Press, New York, 1988.

22   Brecher, Michael, *The Foreign Policy System of Israel: Setting, Images, Process*, Yale University Press, New Haven, 1972.

23   Bregman, Ahron and el-Tahri, Jihan, *The Fifty Years War: Israel and the Arabs*, Penguin Books/BBC Books, 1998.

24   Brown, L. Carl, 'Origins of the crisis', in Richard Parker, *The Six-Day War: A Retrospective*, University Press of Florida, Gainesville, 1996.

25   Brynen, Rex, *Sanctuary and Survival: The PLO in Lebanon*, Westview Press, Boulder, 1990.

26   Caplan, Neil, *Futile Diplomacy, Volume I: Early Arab–Zionist Negotiation Attempts, 1913–1931*, Frank Cass, 1983.

27   Caplan, Neil, *Futile Diplomacy, Volume II: Arab–Zionist Negotiations and the End of the Mandate*, Frank Cass, 1986.

28   Cobban, Helena, *The Palestine Liberation Organization: People, Power, and Policies*, Cambridge University Press, 1984.

29   Cohen, Michael J., *Palestine: Retreat from the Mandate: The Making of British Policy, 1936–1945*, Paul Elek, 1978.

30   Cohen, Michael J., *The Origins and Evolution of the Arab–Israeli Conflict*, University of California Press, 1987.

31   Cohen, Raymond, *Culture and Conflict in Egyptian–Israeli Relations: A Dialogue of the Deaf*, Indiana University Press, Bloomington, 1990.

32   Corbin, Jane, *The Norway Channel: The Secret Talks that led to the Middle East Peace Accord*, Atlantic Monthly Press, New York, 1994.

33   Dayan, Moshe, *Diary of the Sinai Campaign 1956*, Sphere Books, 1967.

34   Dayan, Moshe, *Breakthrough: A Personal Account of the Egypt–Israel Peace Negotiations*, Knopf, New York, 1981.

35   Drezon–Tepler, Marcia, *Interest Groups and Political Change in Israel*, State University of New York Press, Albany, 1990.

36   Dumper, Michael, *The Politics of Jerusalem since 1967*, Columbia University Press, New York, 1997.

37   Eban, Abba, *Personal Witness: Israel through My Eyes*, Jonathan Cape, 1992.

38   Eden, Anthony, *The Suez Crisis of 1956*, Beacon Press, Boston, 1968.

39 Eisenberg, Laura Z., *My Enemy's Enemy: Lebanon in Early Zionist Imagination 1900–1948*, Wayne State University Press, Detroit, 1994.
40 Eisenhower, Dwight D., *The White House Years: Waging Peace, 1956–61*, Doubleday, Garden City, New York, 1965.
41 Evron, Yair, *The Middle East: Nations, Superpowers and Wars*, Praeger, New York, 1973.
42 Evron, Yair, *War and Intervention in Lebanon*, Croom Helm, 1987.
43 Flamhaft, Ziva, 'Israel and the Arab–Israeli peace process in the 1990s' in A. Lazin and Gregory S. Mahler, *Israel in the Nineties: Development and Conflict*, University of Florida Press, Gainesville, 1996.
44 Flamhaft, Ziva, *Israel on the Road to Peace: Accepting the Unacceptable*, Westview Press, Boulder, 1996.
45 Flapan, Simha, *The Birth of Israel: Myths and Realities*, Pantheon Books, New York, 1987.
46 Ford, Gerald, *A Time to Heal*, Allen, 1979.
47 Fraser, T.G., *The Arab–Israeli Conflict*, St Martin's Press, New York, 1995.
48 Freedman, Robert O., *The Intifada: Its Impact on Israel, the Arab World, and the Superpowers*, Florida International University, Miami, 1991.
49 Gabriel, Richard, *Operation Peace for Galilee: The Israel–PLO War in Lebanon*, Hill and Wang, New York, 1984.
50 Garfinkle, Adam, *Politics and Society in Modern Israel: Myths and Realities*, M.E. Sharpe, 1997.
51 Gerges, Fawaz A., *The Superpowers and the Middle East: Regional and International Politics, 1955–1967*, Westview Press, Boulder, 1994.
52 Golan, Galia, *Moscow and the Middle East: New Thinking on Regional Conflict*, Council on Foreign Relations Press, New York, 1992.
53 Golani, Motti, 'The historical place of the Czech–Egyptian arms deal, fall 1955', *Middle Eastern Studies*, Vol. 31, No. 4, October 1995.
54 Goldschmidt, Arthur Jr, *A Concise History of the Middle East*, 5th edition, Westview Press, Boulder, 1996.
55 Greffenius, Steven, *The Logic of Conflict: Making War and Peace in the Middle East*, Sharpe, Armonk, 1993.
56 Gresh, Alain, *The PLO: The Struggle Within: Towards an Independent Palestinian State*, Zed Books,1988.
57 Hadari, Ze'ev Venia, *Second Exodus: The Full Story of Jewish Illegal Immigration to Palestine, 1945–1948*, Valentine, Mitchell, 1991.
58 Harris, William, *Faces of Lebanon: Sects, Wars and Global Extensions*, Marcus Wiener, Princeton, 1997.
59 Heikal, Mohamed H., *The Cairo Documents: The Inside Story of Nasser and his Relationships with World Leaders*, Doubleday, New York, 1973.
60 Heikal, Mohamed H., *The Road to Ramadan*, Balantine, New York, 1977.

61   Heikal, Mohamed H., *The Sphinx and the Commissar: The Rise and Fall of Soviet Influence in the Middle East*, Harper & Row, New York, 1978.

62   Heikal, Mohamed H., *Autumn of Fury: The Assassination of Sadat*, Random House, New York, 1983.

63   Heikal, Mohamed H., *Cutting the Lion's Tail: Suez through Egyptian Eyes*, Andre Deutsch, 1986.

64   Heller, Mark, *A Palestinian State: The Implications for Israel*, Harvard University Press, Cambridge, Mass., 1983.

65   Hopwood, Derek, *Egypt: Politics and Society, 1945–90*, 3rd edition, Routledge, 1991.

66   Hudson, Michael C., *Arab Politics: The Search for Legitimacy*, Yale University Press, New Haven, 1977.

67   Hunter, Robert F., *The Palestinian Uprising: A War by Other Means* (2nd edition), University of California Press, Berkeley, 1993.

68   Jansen, Michael, *The Battle of Beirut: Why Israel invaded Lebanon*, Zed Press, 1982.

69   Karsh, Efraim. 'Rewriting Israel's History', *Middle East Quarterly*, June 1996.

70   Karsh, Efraim, *Fabricating Israeli History: The 'New Historians'*, Frank Cass, 1997.

71   Kimche, David, *The Last Option*, Weidenfeld & Nicolson, 1991.

72   King, John, *Handshake in Washington: The Beginning of Middle East Peace?*, Ithaca Press, Garnet Publishing, 1994.

73   Kissinger, Henry, *Years of Upheaval*, Little, Brown, Boston, 1982.

74   Klieman, Aaron, *Statecraft in the Dark: Israel's Practice of Quiet Diplomacy*, Westview Press, Boulder, 1988.

75   Kyle, Keith, *Suez*, St Martin's Press, New York, 1991.

76   Lall, Arthur S., *The UN and the Middle East Crisis, 1967*, Columbia University Press, New York, 1968.

77   Laqueur, Walter (ed.), *The Israel–Arab Reader: A Documentary History of the Middle East Conflict*, Bantam Books, 1968.

78   Laqueur, Walter, *A History of Zionism: From the French Revolution to the Establishment of the State of Israel*, MFJ Books, New York, 1972.

79   Laqueur, Walter, *Confrontation: The Middle East and World Politics*, New York Times Books, New York, 1974.

80   Lesch, Ann Mosely, *Arab Politics in Palestine, 1917–1939: The Frustration of a Nationalist Movement*, Cornell University Press, Ithaca, 1979.

81   Lesch, Ann Mosely, 'The Palestinian uprising – causes and consequences', *United Field Staff International Reports*, Asia, No. 1, 1988–89.

82   Levey, Zach, 'Anglo–Israeli strategic relations, 1952–56', *Middle Eastern Studies*, Vol. 31, No.4, October 1995.

83   Lipson, Charles, 'American support for Israel: history, sources, limits', *Israel Affairs*, Vol. 2, Nos 3&4, Spring/Summer 1996.

84 Lockman, Zachary and Beinin, Joel, *Intifada: The Palestinian Uprising against Israeli Occupation*, I.B.Tauris, 1989.

85 MacBride, Sean, *Israel in Lebanon: The Report of the International Commission to enquire into reported violations of International Law by Israel during its invasion of Lebanon*, Ithaca Press, 1983.

86 McDowell, David, *Palestine and Israel: The Uprising and Beyond*, I.B.Tauris, 1989.

87 Al-Madfai, Rashid, *Jordan, the United States and the Middle East Peace Process, 1974–1991*, Cambridge University Press, 1993.

88 Medzini, Meron, *Israel's Foreign Relations, 1979–80*, Ministry of Foreign Affairs, Jerusalem, 1984.

89 Meir, Golda, *My Life: The Autobiography of Golda Meir*, Futura Publications Ltd, Aylesbury, 1975.

90 Mishal, Shaul, *The PLO under Arafat: Between Gun and Olive Branch*, Yale University Press, New Haven, 1986.

91 Mishal, Shaul and Sela, Avraham, *Hamas: A Behavioral Profile*, Tel Aviv, The Tami Steinmetz Center for Peace Research, 1997.

92 Morris, Benny, *The Birth of the Palestinian Refugee Problem, 1947–1949*, Cambridge University Press, Cambridge, 1987.

93 Morris, Benny, *1948 and After: Israel and the Palestinians*, Oxford University Press, Oxford, 1990.

94 Morris, Benny, *Israel's Border Wars, 1949–1956*, Clarendon Press, Oxford, 1993.

95 Netanyahu, Benjamin, *A Place Among Nations: Israel and the World*, Bantam Books, New York, 1993.

96 Newman, David (ed.), *The Impact of Gush Emunim: Politics and Settlement in the West Bank*, St Martin's Press, New York, 1985.

97 O'Neil, Bard E., *Armed Struggle in Palestine: A Politico-Military Analysis*, Westview Press, Boulder, 1978.

98 Oren, Michael, *The Origins of the second Arab–Israeli War: Egypt, Israel and the Great Powers, 1952–56*, Frank Cass, 1992.

99 Ovendale, Ritchie, *The Origins of the Arab–Israeli Wars* (2nd edition), Longman, 1992.

100 Pappé, Ilan, *The Making of the Arab–Israeli Conflict, 1947–1951*, I.B. Tauris, 1994.

101 Parker, Richard, *The Six-Day War: A Retrospective*, University Press of Florida, Gainesville, 1996.

102 Peleg, Ilan, *Begin's Foreign Policy, 1977–83: Israel's Move to the Right*, Greenwood Press, New York, 1987.

103 Peres, Shimon, *Battling for Peace: A Memoir, Random House*, New York, 1995.

104 Peretz, Don, *The Arab–Israel Dispute*, Facts on File, New York, 1996.

105 Peri, Yoram, *Between Battles and Ballots: Israeli Military in Politics*, Cambridge University Press, Cambridge, 1983.

106 Peri, Yoram, 'Coexistence or hegemony? Shifts in the Israeli security concept', in Dan Caspi, Abraham Diskin, and Emanuel Gutman (eds),

The Roots of Begin's Success: The 1981 Israeli Elections, Croom Helm, 1984.

107 Picard, Elizabeth, *Lebanon: A Shattered Country*, Holmes & Meier, 1996.

108 Rabie, Mohamed, *US–PLO Dialogue: Secret Diplomacy and Conflict Resolution, University Press of Florida*, Gainesville, 1995.

109 Rabinovich, Itamar, *The War for Lebanon, 1970–1985* (revised edition), Cornell University Press, New York, 1985.

110 Rabinovich, Itamar, *The Road not Taken: Early Arab–Israeli Negotiations*, Oxford University Press, New York, 1991.

111 Rabinovich, Itamar and Reinharz, Yehuda, *Israel in the Middle East*, Oxford University Press, Oxford, 1984.

112 Rubin, Barry, 'Iraq and the PLO: brother's keepers, losers weepers', in Amatzia Baram and Barry Rubin (eds), *Iraq's Road to War*, St Martin's Press, New York, 1993.

113 Rubin, Barry, 'The United States and Iraq: from appeasement to war', in Amatzia Baram and Barry Rubin (eds), *Iraq's Road to War*, St Martin's Press, New York, 1993.

114 Safran, Nadav, *From War to War: The Arab–Israeli Confrontation, 1948–1967*, Pegasus, Indianapolis, 1969.

115 Safran, Nadav, *Israel: The Embattled Ally*, Harvard University Press, Cambridge, 1978.

116 Said, Edward W., *The Question of Palestine*, Vintage, 1992.

117 Said, Edward W., *The Politics of Dispossession: The Struggle for Palestinian Self-Determination 1969–1994*, Chatto & Windus, 1994.

118 Sayigh, Yezid, *Arab Military Industry: Capability, Performance, and Impact*, Brassey's, 1992.

119 Sayigh, Yezid and Shlaim, Avi (eds), *The Cold War and the Middle East*, Clarendon Press, Oxford, 1997.

120 Schiff, Zeev, *A History of the Israeli Army*, Sidgwick & Jackson, 1987.

121 Schiff, Zeev, 'Israel after the war', *Foreign Affairs*, 70, Spring 1991.

122 Schiff, Zeev and Ya'ari, Ehud, *Israel's Lebanon War*, George Allen & Unwin, 1984.

123 Schiff, Zeev and Ya'ari, Ehud, *Intifada: The Palestinian Uprising – Israel's Third Front*, Simon and Schuster, 1989.

124 Schulze, Kirsten E., *Israel's Covert Diplomacy in Lebanon*, Macmillan, 1998.

125 Shalev, Aryeh, *Israel and Syria: Peace and Security on the Golan*, Westview Press, Boulder, 1994.

126 Sharett, Moshe, *Yoman Ishi* (Personal Diary), 8 volumes, Sifriyat Maariv, Tel Aviv, 1978.

127 Shemesh, Moshe, *The Palestinian Entity 1959–1974: Arab Politics and the PLO*, Frank Cass, 1988.

128 Shlaim, Avi, *Collusion across the Jordan: King Abdullah, the Zionist Movement, and the Partition of Palestine*, Clarendon Press, Oxford, 1988.

129 Shlaim, Avi, 'Israeli interference in internal Arab affairs: the case of Lebanon' in Giacomo Luciani and Ghassan Salame (eds), *The Politics of Arab Integration*, Croom Helm, 1988.

130 Shlaim, Avi, 'The Debate about 1948', *International Journal for Middle East Studies*, 27, 1995.

131 Smith, Charles D., *Palestine and the Arab–Israeli Conflict* (3rd edition), St Martin's Press, New York, 1996.

132 Sofer, Sasson, *Begin: An Anatomy of Leadership*, Oxford University Press, Oxford, 1988.

133 Sprinzak, Ehud, *The Ascendance of Israel's Radical Right*, Oxford University Press, Oxford, 1991.

134 Stein, Kenneth W., *The Land Question in Palestine, 1917–1939*, University of North Carolina Press, Chapel Hill, 1984.

135 Tamari, Salim, 'The Palestinian movement in transition: historical reversals and the uprising' in Rex Brynen (ed.), *Echoes of the Intifada: Regional Repercussions of the Palestinian–Israeli Conflict*, Westview Press, Boulder, 1991.

136 Tessler, Mark, *History of the Israeli–Palestinian Conflict*, Indiana University Press, Bloomington, 1994.

137 Teveth, Shabtai, *Ben Gurion and the Palestinian Arabs: From Peace to War*, Oxford University Press, Oxford, 1985.

138 Troen, Selwyn Ilan, and Shemesh, Moshe (eds), *The Suez–Sinai Crisis, 1956: Retrospective and Reappraisal*, Frank Cass, 1990.

139 Victor, Barbara, *Hanan Ashrawi: A Passion for Peace*, Fourth Estate, 1995.

140 Weizman, Ezer, *The Battle for Peace*, Bantam Books, 1981.

141 Wells, Samuel F. Jr, 'The Clinton Administration and regional security: the first two years', *Israel Affairs*, Vol. 2, Nos 3&4, Spring/Summer 1996.

142 Yaniv, Avner, *Dilemmas of Security: Politics, Strategy and the Israeli Experience in Lebanon*, Oxford University Press, Oxford, 1987.

143 Yaniv, Avner (ed.), *National Security and Democracy in Israel*, Lynne Rienner, Boulder, 1993.

144 Yapp, Malcom, *The Near East since the First World War*, Longman, 1991.

145 Zartman, I. William, *Ripe for Resolution: Conflict and Intervention in Africa*, Oxford University Press, Oxford, 1989.

146 Zartman, I. William (ed.), *Elusive Peace: Negotiating an End to Civil Wars*, The Brookings Institution, Washington DC, 1995.

147 Zweig, Ronald W., *Britain and Palestine during the Second World War*, Boydell Press, Suffolk, 1986.

INDEX

956.04 SCU.